Will a Frenchman Fight?

Deeds of Arms Series Volume 4

Will a Frenchman Fight?

Translated and Edited by Steven Muhlberger

Freelance Academy Press, Inc.
www.FreelanceAcademyPress.com

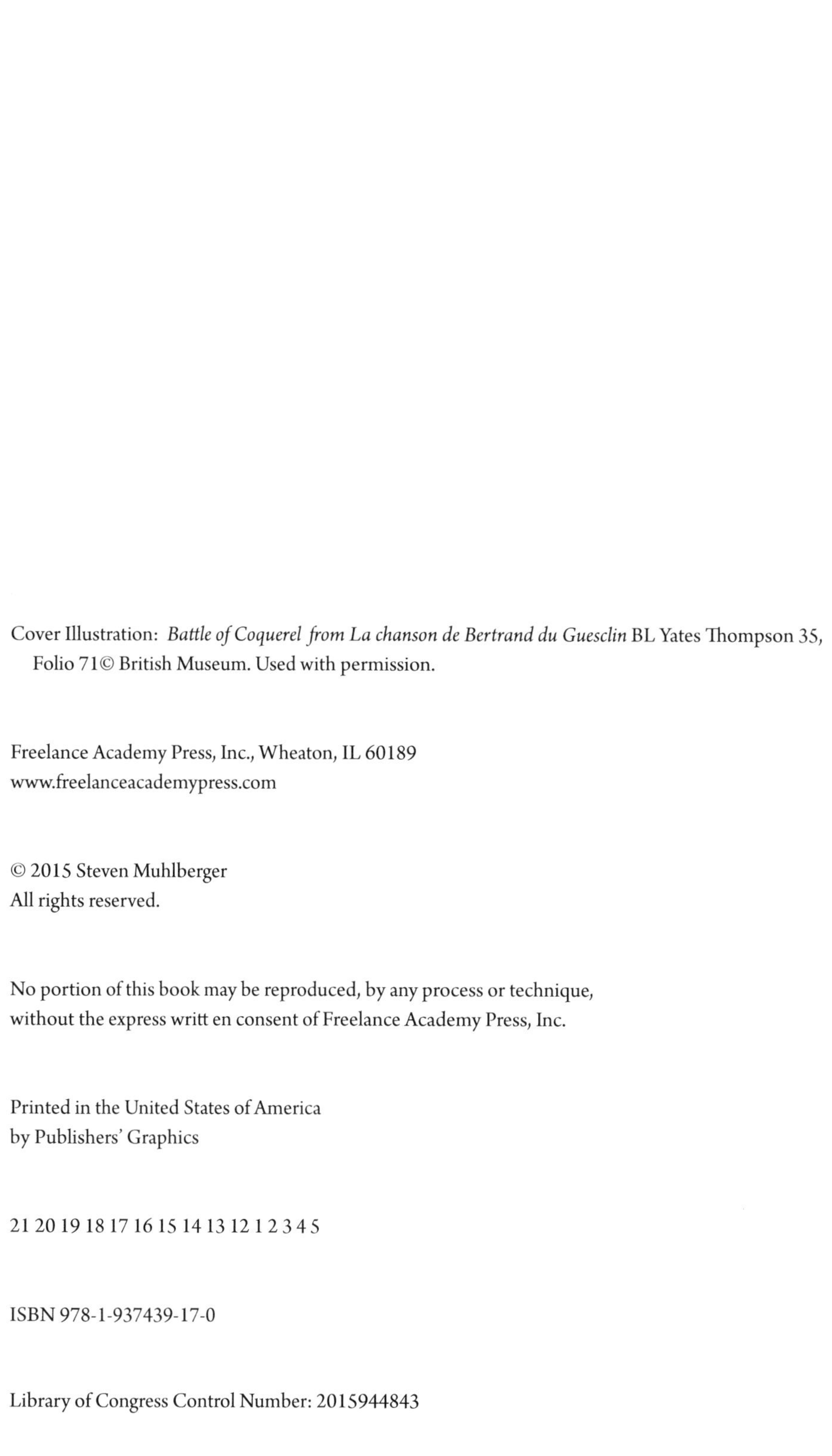

Cover Illustration: *Battle of Coquerel from La chanson de Bertrand du Guesclin* BL Yates Thompson 35, Folio 71© British Museum. Used with permission.

Freelance Academy Press, Inc., Wheaton, IL 60189
www.freelanceacademypress.com

Printed in the United States of America
by Publishers' Graphics

21 20 19 18 17 16 15 14 13 12 1 2 3 4 5

ISBN 978-1-937439-17-0

Library of Congress Control Number: 2015944843

Contents

List of Illustrations

Will a Frenchman Fight?

Chivalric Combat and Practical Warfare in the Hundred Years War

Steven Muhlberger

Introduction

It's a truism that individual soldiers fight for different reasons than their leaders do. Modern soldiers often fight for their friends first and the cause second. In the past, it was common for the individual to fight for his own glory and reputation. This is often taken as a defining feature of "chivalric warfare."[1] *Will a Frenchman Fight?* describes a campaign of the Hundred Years War in 1380–1 in which a variety of different kinds of combat and different motives for fighting are evident. The campaign itself was a great *chevauchée*, or raid, by the English through France and though it had its practical goals, it was also a striking illustration of the place of chivalric self-image in shaping warfare. The English hoped to weaken their opponents by demonstrating that the French king, Charles V, could not defend his subjects. The French king had practical reasons for wishing to avoid spectacular but dangerous set battles similar to Crecy and Poitiers—battles that had been catastrophic for the French. Avoiding battle, however, had its price. If enough people in France concluded that the English were right in their scorn for royal power, that power would be significantly reduced.

Frustrated Kings and Warlords in the 1380s

The rulers of both England and France had reason to be unhappy as the 1380s dawned. Although the French regime was in better shape than it had been in a while, the country still lay open to English attack and the populace was angry about it. The English regime was no happier; it was futilely trying to realize the

1 See the bibliography for some of the most important recent scholarly works on the nature and development of chivalry and its relationship to war.

gains seemingly promised by the victory at Poitiers back in 1356. This had been its constant occupation for a quarter century, but ultimate success seemed as far away as ever.

Following Poitiers and the capture and ransoming of King Jean II, the English and the French courts had negotiated a sweeping treaty at Bretigny in 1359. On the face of it, the treaty put the seal on an English victory of unprecedented extent. It granted the King of England huge territories on the continent and promised that in short order his possessions would be free and clear of any duty to his French neighbor.

It soon became clear that the English had overreached themselves. Their astonishing victory had won them an impressive legal title to Gascony and southwestern France, but their power was more precarious than it appeared. New strains revealed the hidden weakness. Edward the Prince of Wales, the hero of Poitiers, quickly transformed himself from beloved champion to oppressive overlord when he began raising unprecedented taxes in Gascony to finance an invasion of Castile. The invasion was a success, but again profit did not follow victory. Prince Edward's subjects in Gascony quickly became disillusioned and began to look to Paris for support against English rule. In 1369, Charles V found a legal excuse for repudiating the treaty of Bretigny and began a long-term campaign to recover the territory France had just ceded.

Slowly, England began losing ground. Defending all existing gains was expensive, and the war was now a liability rather than a rallying point. The political class of England did not quite understand why military success had not resulted in a happier economic situation. It did not help that after the Black Death (1347–50, 1361–2) the institutions of the past no longer worked as they once had. Whenever the landlords of England gathered in Parliament and were asked by King Edward III's ministers to pay for a new campaign, they got cranky, even though many of them were experienced warriors whom one might expect to appreciate how expensive war was. Furthermore, the generals of the new generation were either not as good or not as lucky as Edward III and his son Prince Edward, who had become disabled by age and illness respectively and were not available to lead the armies. Other English leaders worked very hard to duplicate the successes of old, but in vain.

Although the period between the treaty of 1359 and 1380 can be seen as one full of English setbacks, France still suffered significantly and the political position of the court was fragile. Following the defeat at Poitiers, France had been torn by a series of conflicts and disasters: the destruction of much of the fighting aristocracy at the battle itself; the revolt known as the *Jacquerie*, in which the peasants rose up against what they saw as an ineffective aristocratic warrior class who no longer deserved their position; and the revolt of the people of Paris—the single most important lordship of the French king—which was also inspired by disgust with the royal government and the aristocracy. Charles V, Jean's heir and regent during the king's captivity (1356–60), was able to re-establish royal authority, and when he succeeded his father he was, as we have seen, able to start recovering territory. Nevertheless, France was repeatedly attacked by England and overrun by outlaws and disbanded mercenaries, even when there was no English army in the field.

Charles' actions and initiatives were cautious ones. This is particularly evident in the way he handled the various invasions of France between 1370 and 1380. The English clearly had a superior tactical doctrine and facing them in battle was not a risk that a prudent leader would take—or so Charles reasoned. The aftermath of Poitiers was always hovering before his eyes. Better by far to avoid battle, to harass English armies as they marched through France, and wait until lack of supplies and the disease that always manifested itself in medieval campaigns forced the army to withdraw to English bastions like Calais. As Charles said to his captains, "Let them alone: they will destroy themselves."

As we have said, it was a prudent strategy. But its inherent weakness is shown by the fact that Charles's own captains found it unsatisfying, perhaps dishonorable. Prudence and practicality were military virtues that were highly thought of, but boldness, courage, and the ability to win a straightforward battle against one's opponent were regarded even more highly. Readers familiar with the *Song of Roland* will remember how the hero's companion Olivier speaks eloquently for common sense, in this case for not being too proud to call for reinforcements. Clearly poet and audience understood the points he made; nevertheless, Roland remains the hero and the poem is the *Song of Roland* and not the *Song of Olivier*. Those involved in the Hundred Years War were strongly attached to the idea of personal prowess, and collective prowess as well. They evaluated their own performance and the performance of their enemies in war in much the same way as they did a performance of the joust or a chivalric deed of arms. In such deeds, a warrior committed himself to fulfilling a certain set of military exercises. We will see later Frenchmen proposing to fight an equal number of English warriors to the death or to capture, without any possibility of running away. We will also read about English and French committing to exchanging equal blows, "five blows of the lance, five of the sword, five of the axe, five of the dagger." To make such commitments and then fail to carry them out was a disgrace. To avoid a decisive engagement was also a blot on the individual or on the army, and seemed to show insufficient courage. Those who were vulnerable to criticism were keenly aware of what other people might be saying about them.

The prelude to the great joust at St. Inglevert in 1390, about a decade after the events discussed in this book, illustrates how deeds of arms and practical warfare were regulated by similar considerations of honor. At that later time, England and France were at truce and prospects for a lasting peace looked good. Yet at the level of the individual warrior, at least the more aristocratic ones, bragging rights were still hotly contested. English knights, taking advantage of their newfound ability to tour France in peace, could not resist baiting Frenchmen they met with the memory of great English victories. Such bragging stung. Three young but experienced Frenchmen, members of the king's household, responded by proposing a great jousting meet where they would demonstrate the superiority of the French for everyone to see. More cautious members of the royal entourage were alarmed by the prospect of this public challenge, believing that even a friendly series of jousts would lead to heated tempers and endanger the truce. Cooler heads prevailed and the joust was redefined as a challenge to the entire chivalric world and not specifically the English. The incident shows how considerations of war, peace and personal honor were tightly bound together, and that direct confrontation of man against man or army against army was the most satisfying way of settling such issues.

Buckingham's Campaign of 1380-1

On the English side, Buckingham's chevauchée, the great raid that is our focus here, is often considered somewhat insignificant; one short history of the Hundred Years War devotes a mere half-sentence to it. On the French side, the military action is somewhat overshadowed by contemporary events far from the battlefield, such as the deaths of the French Constable, Bertrand du Guesclin and King Charles V, the battles between dukes over the regency thereafter, and the complexities of the relationship between Jean de Montfort, duke of Brittany, and the royal government. Yet Buckingham's expedition was a major effort on the part of the English government to extend and solidify its control over French territory: so major that the taxation associated with it helped cause the English Peasants' Revolt (May-November, 1381). The French government likewise faced revolt from a population, which suffered from rising taxation in a time of demographic and economic decline. The most recent narrative history of the war, by Jonathan Sumption, includes more material on the politics of parliamentary resistance to royal demands in both countries than to the details of the campaign of 1380–1; there are good reasons for that choice.

Yet the chronicler Jean Froissart, who wrote a contemporary account of Buckingham's campaign, thought it worthy of a very detailed accounting. He featured as much the deeds of arms accomplished by named individuals as he did the movements of armies. Indeed the campaign can be seen, in his telling, as a context for tests of chivalry performed by both English and French men-at-arms, who serve as representatives of the virtues and vices of their fellow countrymen. The campaign becomes a competition of honor (that is, the gaining of respect), played out on two levels, the macro and micro—a competition which, in Froissart's opinion, was won by the French.

Fifty years after Froissart wrote, another French chronicler, Cabaret d'Orville, presented a similar evaluation of Buckingham's campaign in the *Chronicle of the Good Duke*. This 1429 work was derived from the reminiscences of a participant in the campaign, Jean de Châteaumorand, who also took part in the most prominent formal deed of arms associated with Buckingham's chevauchée, the deed at Vannes. Châteaumorand, still alive in 1429, provided the chronicler an account independent of Froissart's but similar in its emphasis on French honor and how it was upheld on the macro and micro levels. Even a half-century on, a chief concern of the composer of the *Chronicle* was to show that when challenged, Frenchmen would indeed fight, fight well and fight successfully, according to the best standards of chivalric behavior. Would a Frenchman fight? Yes. More interesting than the predictable answer is the fact that the question had to be asked and answered at all. Before we explore this, however, we need to put Buckingham's campaign into a strategic context.

Buckingham's March to Brittany

The English had a long-standing interest in detaching Brittany from the court of Paris. Brittany was one of the closest parts of the continent to England, and it could not be avoided by anyone wishing to sail from England to its rich possessions in Gascony. In some eras, Brittany may have been an isolated region, but now it was quite central. Paris and London competed for dominance and dynastic complexities added to the chaotic political situation. Two branches of the ducal family had claimed the right to rule after the death of the childless Duke Jean (III) in 1341. Both rivals had early on turned to the rival kings for help. England supported the Montfort branch while the French court supported the Blois. The famous Combat of the Thirty illustrates the indecisiveness of the competition, and the effect of war between pro-French and pro-English garrisons on the fabric of Breton society. A very important and easily overlooked aspect of that combat of 1351 is that Bretons fought on both sides, and that Breton loyalty to the ruler whom a Breton poet called "the King of Saint-Denis"(implying that he ruled only in suburban Paris, where the famous basilica and abbey associated with the French crown were) could not be taken for granted.

By the 1370s, Jean de Montfort (V) had something of an advantage, thanks to the fact that his main rival was an English prisoner. Nevertheless, his position was still weak, and he had been forced into exile. In 1378 Charles V had made enough progress in other fronts of his war of consolidation to be able to move against Jean. Jean was summoned to answer charges of treason, and when he quite sensibly did not show up for his trial, he was condemned in absentia and his duchy confiscated.

The confidence Charles V showed in undertaking these actions was quite misplaced. Jean de Montfort had not been a popular duke, and many of the most important nobles had been sympathetic to the French cause. Yet, these nobles had no desire to be directly ruled from Paris. It is indicative of Charles's miscalculation that he could only with difficulty command the obedience of some of his own key military leaders who were Bretons themselves, despite their hatred for Jean de Montfort. Indeed, resentment of the royal coup flared up very quickly and a league of resistance was formed in April of 1379. Montfort's formerly disloyal subjects invited him back to lead the resistance and take his place as duke.

Jean de Montfort's first thought was to negotiate with the English for an army to support his power independent of his unreliable subjects, but when a cash-strapped English government did not act quickly on his request, Jean went back without an army—a very risky move that nonetheless succeeded. Distracted by other problems, the French were unable to respond. A truce was struck in October of 1379, which gave Jean time to secure his alliance with England. This alliance made Buckingham's expedition to France possible.

The original plan for Buckingham's attack was to cross to Brittany and use it as a starting point from which the combined forces of England and de Montfort could attack northern France or, more likely, head south to reinforce the English garrison in Gascony. This soon proved impossible; English shipping had declined to the point that an entire army could not be transported to Brittany from England in one go. Rather it had to cross bit by bit in barges over the narrow seas at Calais. That meant that Buckingham could join de Montfort only after marching a well-worn route around Paris and then west to Brittany. I doubt that anyone objected to this difficult prologue to the main campaign. Major raids or chevauchées of this sort, aimed at the heartland of French royal power, had been a standard English tactic since the 1340s, and similar chevauchées had taken place in 1370 and 1373. Such a march might provoke the French into once again fighting a battle against superior English tactics, or at least weaken French royal power and prestige. No one seems to have pointed out that even the most successful past chevauchée, the one that ended at Poitiers in 1356 with the capture of the French king, had not produced an overall victory for England.

Buckingham's march from Calais to Brittany began in July of 1380. The strategy King Charles insisted upon for the French was one that had proved successful in the 1370s, if at a cost. French troops holed up in garrisons, while others followed the English army closely enough to deny them easy access to fodder and plunder. The cost was borne, materially, by the rural population, and psychically by the French warriors who, anxious to show their worthiness, wished to fight the invaders. Charles's understanding that a marching English army would destroy itself was no crank theory: its validity had been amply demonstrated. But this was no help to those whose property was destroyed or whose reputation suffered because of their forced inactivity. How well the French military aristocracy performed their God-given duty to defend the realm had long been a controversial topic in French politics. Those who paid taxes for protection expected to get it and bitterly complained, and indeed went beyond mere complaint, when they did not. Nor could they respect a royal government that was constantly extorting higher taxes but not using them in any obvious way to stop such attacks as Buckingham's. It must have looked like sheer incompetence or perhaps misfeasance.

Aristocrats and warriors must have been infuriated to hear of criticism by non-fighters of their unwillingness to engage the enemy when they were perfectly willing to do so. Yet I suspect that criticism, imagined or real, which came from other warriors hurt them much more. The willingness to engage in the dangerous and laborious life of arms not only justified the privileges of the warrior, it was an essential part of his social and personal identity. The strain which Charles's common-sense strategy imposed on the inner Roland of every French warrior can be seen in words Froissart attributed to the lord of Couci, one of the chief French commanders: "It is then clear that they [the English] wish for battle; which they shall have, if the king our lord will trust us, before they have finished their march."

The royal permission never came. Even when the English army faced a large French force at Troyes, no battle resulted. The English continued to march, and the French to make trouble for them. In mid-September, the death of Charles V resulted in the temporary collapse of French initiative. There was no money to pay the troops, some of whom were demobilized and some of whom just went home on their own. The great dukes to whom the initiative fell were entirely distracted by the question of who would control the government of the new child-king, Charles VI. This allowed the English earl to proceed to Brittany without meeting much opposition.

When he reached the duchy, however, the earl found a major disappointment. The duke of Brittany had assembled no army nor made any provisions for supplying his English allies. When the duke finally appeared for consultations he refused to be pinned down. Jean de Montfort was keeping a close eye on developments in Paris. He calculated that with Charles V gone, it would be possible to make peace with the court. The English alliance was now going to be a disadvantage. While he secretly reached out to Paris, the duke agreed with Buckingham on a plan according to which the English army and a Breton one— which probably did not exist—would attempt to take the city of Nantes, which was both defying ducal authority and which was the site of the bridge that Buckingham needed to cross if he were to take his army south towards Gascony. Before the English got to Nantes, however, the leadership in Paris woke up momentarily and put 600 soldiers into the city. One of the commanders charged with the defense was our source, Jean de Châteaumorand.

Buckingham was stalled militarily and politically at Nantes. The city was well fortified and well positioned to defend itself. The 600 French troops, even though they were very much outnumbered, were able to deter English assaults, and in contrast to their behavior earlier in Buckingham's march, take the initiative. The English battalions were separated by rivers and terrain and could not cooperate easily. The French defenders, on the other hand, were able to work from their central position and launch a number of dramatic and successful raids on the English siege camps. More daunting for the English than even these attacks was the usual medieval killer of armies, dysentery (the "stomach flux"). As winter came on, the English suffered terribly from the weather and by January 6, the earl of Buckingham had found it impossible to continue the siege and withdrew from before the city to a number of smaller camps. Despite the fact that the English had had a sizable army in French territory during a time when the French government was in complete chaos, the usual conditions of fourteenth-century military campaigning had effectively defeated them. The royal government in London, far from the action, still nursed a hope that reinforcements and more money would save the campaign, but the earl and his experienced commanders knew the jig was up. The English leaders began negotiating with their enemies for funds to finance a withdrawal to England by sea. An agreement was reached in March setting terms for that withdrawal.

The end of the great chevauchée was marked by one of the most famous deeds of arms recorded by Froissart, the foot combats between French and English champions at Vannes. As Jonathan Sumption has remarked, these combats did not go well for the English, either. Buckingham spent the next month merely waiting for money to leave Brittany, which he did in early May. Nothing had been achieved except the alienation of the English taxpayer, which was so severe that in late May, the commoners of England began the greatest uprising of the Middle Ages.

Deeds of Arms, Individual and Collective

Two French narratives of the campaign of 1380–1 exist. Both work hard to demonstrate not just the fact of French victory, but the worthiness of French behavior. They rebuff the idea that the French defeated Buckingham in unworthy avoidance of manly and chivalric combat. There is good evidence that unfavorable views of French behavior existed. In his account of the campaign, the English chronicler Walsingham presented the story as one of cowardice and the sort of bad faith that was so typical of the French. Neither the French king nor his dukes were able to face Buckingham's army. The French refused battle on a number of occasions, notably at Troyes. When the earl of Buckingham marched to meet the duke of Brittany, his supposed ally, he found more treachery: while English men-at-arms suffered in the duke's cause, he had been negotiating with the French government. But we actually don't need Walsingham to reconstruct the failure of French chivalry. The efforts of Froissart and Cabaret to provide a different narrative, one that by showing the chivalric qualities of the French and how the English repeatedly fell short of those standards, allows us to imagine contemporary criticism of French performance.

Partisanship is strong in the version of the tale that originated with Jean de Châteaumorand, who was a lifelong enemy of the English. In 1429, when the English dominated a defeated France, he provided Cabaret with stories of old victories over a hated enemy. He has no sentimentality or fellow feeling for the English. His picture is one of sharp contrast between the two nationalities. Froissart, if somewhat milder, is equally clear in showing the difference between English and French. From his very detailed account two issues emerge: Who among the combatants was as good as their word? Furthermore, were the French willing to fight or no?

Willingness to fight and fulfilling an enterprise or commitment (*emprise*) were practically the definition of a good man-at-arms' duty and way of life. Châteaumorand provided Cabaret with an anecdotal demonstration of chivalry from the good old days by means of a story which concerned a Savoyard bastard named Clarins, who was one of Châteaumorand's fellow participants in the deeds of Vannes. During a siege in 1375, Clarins became irritated by a Gascon in the English garrison who was constantly accusing a French lord of breach of faith and threatening violent retribution. Although there was no connection between the Frenchman and Clarins, Clarins took up his cause. He challenged the English accuser because he thought it was the right thing to do:

> If you are as good at fighting as you say, tomorrow I will fight you before my lord the duke of Bourbon, on condition that if I defeat you, you will be my prisoner and if you defeat me, I will be yours. You should not refuse me this if you want to fight, for this is the profession of arms. **(CBD 98)**

The challenge was accepted, and Clarins thrashed and nearly killed the mouthy Gascon. It was an episode worth remembering a half-century later, for it expressed a standard that the French strategy of Charles V did not meet. What Charles wanted of his troops, especially the leaders, was something entirely different—self-restraint in the face of extreme provocation. He demanded that they refuse combat, refuse direct challenges. And how that hurt! In Froissart's account, we repeatedly see the dissatisfaction of the French with their assigned role.

In the early stages of the chevauchée, according to Froissart, the French performed in such a way as to leave them open to English criticism—and perhaps not just English criticism. The English, enthusiastically looking for an opportunity to show their stuff, presented themselves before French strongpoints, hoping that members of the garrison would come out to meet them. Only rarely did the French respond with more than skirmishing over barriers, and some of those who did more met embarrassing defeat. But generally they held back, obeying orders, grinding their teeth, and wishing that they could rebut the implied and express aspersions on their courage. The most important confrontation took place at the city of Troyes, where a large French army under the command of the duke of Burgundy was gathered. Here, if ever, was a brilliant occasion for a major battle and test of chivalry. The English made the most of it, sending the French a formal challenge to meet them in the open field, " in such a way as we ought to meet our enemies." Despite these words and a later challenge where Buckingham, "son of the King of England," demanded battle, Burgundy kept the bulk of his forces behind the walls of the city.

The difficulty in refusing such an open challenge, from one chivalric lord to another, is indicated by the way Froissart goes to great lengths to insist that the heralds sent to Burgundy were not able to get through to him to deliver the messages. In other words, the French duke, and by extension his army, could not fairly be accused of refusing battle. How many people would be convinced by this logic is hard to say, but it was the best that could be offered to the undoubted English view that the French, given the opportunity to answer a direct challenge, had offered the English only a paltry answer.

It is this atmosphere of French shame about their own passivity that gives the story of Gauvain Micaille a particularly important place in the unfolding narrative offered by Froissart. Sometime after the English left Troyes and moved through the region of Beauce, they came before Toury, where one of Charles V's trusted commanders, the lord of Sempy, was holding the position. A certain amount of skirmishing took place between the garrison and the English, until Gauvain Micaille, a French squire, came to the barriers and challenged any Englishman inspired by love of his lady to fight one-on-one against him. Skirmishing halted as the English considered the offer. It was a dramatic moment, specifically because the English "thought this enterprise a great bravado, for they did not believe any Frenchman would dare to fight body to body." This short phrase speaks volumes about how the English viewed the French performance to date. Gauvain's commitment to "body to body" combat was a different matter entirely, the appropriate response of a self-respecting man-at-arms.

The complete story of Gauvain Micaille is told below, but two points are worth noting here. First Gauvain himself seems to have come out of the deed, which took place over two separate days, with good credit, while the English champion put against him performed poorly in the joust, striking Micaille low and piercing his thigh. The result of this confrontation was English anger and disgrace. "The earl of Buckingham as well as the other lords were much enraged by this, and said it was jousting dishonorably." Second, during the second day of the deed, at Marchenoir, circumstances led to the French taking a more active stance. Both English and French men-at-arms were present to watch the deed. There was conversation and some of it was about chivalry. "Words passed" between English and Frenchmen, who were on both sides anxious to prove themselves. The earl of Buckingham, thinking of the military situation, refused to delay his further march to allow these challenges to be fought out immediately. But the challenges remained on the table, to be fulfilled at some later time. The atmosphere cleared for the French. They must have felt that because of Micaille's performance and their own demonstration of willingness to fight that they could hold their heads high.

By the time the English army faced the French garrison at Nantes, the initiative had completely passed over to the French. Froissart and Cabaret (or Châteaumorand) both told colorful stories of French success. (Châteaumorand's recollections had been improved on, so that he claims that he and his friends killed several English bannerets whom we know survived until a later time.) The old man or his interviewer considered the details of the actions around Nantes worthy of a great deal of attention, even though the events were not really relevant to the life of the good duke, who was not present. Froissart makes it clear that the raids that the French made on the English positions were "gallant actions" admired by the people on both sides. Both chroniclers were intent on showing in some detail how French boldness and skill had nullified English efforts.

Vannes

In the winter of 1381, the earl of Buckingham realized that his campaign was a failure and broke the siege. But people on both sides still wanted to fight in order to demonstrate their prowess and determination. According to the chroniclers, there were still outstanding challenges from Marchenoir. Froissart portrays a situation where the chief commanders, like their subordinates, were anxious to show that they were good patrons of chivalry. Buckingham and his counterpart the constable of France competed, for instance, over the issuing of safe conducts so that deeds of arms could take place. What might seem to be solely a practical necessity took on a symbolic weight. The constable of France is shown as acknowledging the earl of Buckingham's right to guarantee the safety of those looking for chivalric adventure—as well he should.

Once arrangements had been made, the earl presided over a carefully defined deed where five Englishmen and English partisans would fight five Frenchmen with lances, swords, axes and daggers, all on foot. The Frenchmen included Jean de Châteaumorand and Clarins the bastard of Savoy. Most of the participants in this deed on either side are pretty well known to modern historians. They were men of experience and prestige, putting their honor on the line in hopes of increasing their renown and, it should not be forgotten, to uphold the honor of the army, their lord, and their comrades. The story of Vannes as told by Froissart is reproduced below, but the key point is that the English did rather badly. Not one but two English combatants performed so poorly that their countrymen withdrew them from the fight. Clarins, whose opponent Edward Beauchamp was the first to withdraw in this fashion, complained bitterly. He insisted that someone else should help him complete his arms. The earl of Buckingham, who was acting as judge and as host to the visiting French men-at-arms, had to admit the justice of this demand, and sent out another opponent who succeeded in giving Clarins a good fight.

Jean de Châteaumorand followed Clarins and fought an English squire named Janikin Clinton, who, like the Edward Beauchamp mentioned above, found himself knocked about by his French opponent. Again the English—in fact the commander/judge/host, Buckingham—pulled out his champion to avoid a humiliating defeat. But by the standard set by Clarins, it traded one kind of disgrace for another. Châteaumorand was in a position to complain that the English were doing him wrong, unless they made it possible for him to fulfill his deed of arms. And another champion was provided, an experienced knight named William Farringdon.

This fight is the most remarkable of all the formal deeds of arms recorded by Froissart, but is not explained very well (Cabaret and Châteaumorand do better). Farringdon and Châteaumorand decided to fight with lances without striking at their limbs, which evidently were unarmored. Farringdon struck too low, thrusting the point of his lance through Châteaumorand's thigh. It was a villainous act, and condemnation rained down on Farringdon's head. That the rest of the English shared in his disgrace was made clear by the fact that they took the lead in denouncing their champion. Eventually, the matter was patched up and the French departed carrying Châteaumorand home in a litter.

Froissart shows the deeds of Vannes as a disaster for the English. The French knocked them up and down the field, twice forcing the English into a choice between abandoning their *emprises* or having champions thoroughly defeated. Of the two types of disgrace, the one they chose was perhaps the worse. Froissart's sketch of the earl of Buckingham is worthy of notice. A king's son and a would-be patron of chivalry, he comes across as an utter failure, even if he is portrayed in polite terms. As a commander and conqueror he had failed. Likewise, his men let him down on what later ages would call the field of honor. At Vannes, as before at Marchenoir, he was forced to apologize for an Englishman who unskillfully broke the implied rules of jousting—on horse or on foot—by striking low and injuring an opponent in an off-target part of the body.

The story of Vannes as filtered through the collections of the wounded Châteaumorand is even harsher in its evaluation of the English performance. Cabaret's account shows English bad faith and laxity from the beginning. The original deed agreed upon by both French and English had been a deed of fifteen against fifteen *á outrance*, in which the combatants would fight until death or capture, with no presiding figure to stop the fight if it went too far. The Earl, using plausible excuses, prevented his men from taking part, and insisted on a limited deed of counted blows. Then, on the day of the deed, the English brought only five men willing to fight. Châteaumorand shows almost clinical interest in recording the injuries suffered by the English, who were overcome in almost every instance. Châteaumorand had a slightly different memory of how he got wounded. It resulted from a challenge that was made at the dinner that followed the morning's five fights. Where Froissart remembers Frenchmen protesting when they were prevented from fulfilling their enterprise, and justifiably so, Cabernet's account shows an unjustifiable complaint rudely brought up during dinner. An English knight, perhaps a retainer of the duke of Brittany, challenged Châteaumorand to finish the deed that the challenger's relative had been unable to finish. There was something very offensive in the way this was done, and the challenge was accepted only because Châteaumorand wanted to fight it out. Arriving at the field the next morning, Châteaumorand found the English knight claiming that he was not able to wear his leg armor, and that he wanted Châteaumorand to do the same. Then, of course, disaster resulted, which was entirely the fault of the Englishman. Once again denunciation rained down upon an English champion, and the earl of Buckingham was put in the position of placating Frenchmen for the fault of his people. This gave Châteaumorand an opportunity to be gracious once more, refusing revenge, refusing a gift of money, and generally demonstrating that men of his sort—retainers of the Good Duke of Bourbon—fought only for worthy and not mercenary motives.

Froissart, writing soon after Buckingham's campaign, with access to a variety of sources, and Cabaret, reflecting Châteaumorand's recollections of what he remembered as a golden age of chivalry under the Good Duke, were agreed on an essential point. Despite doubts about French conduct that various people may have expressed at the time, French chivalry was confirmed by the deeds of arms that took place at Vannes, which served to put a period to the story of the failed chevauchée. If there is any doubt about that conclusion, one need only consider Froissart's final look at the campaign of 1380-1—and an episode where once again an Englishman comes across as lacking finer feeling.

The Deed of Nicholas Clifford and Jean Boucinel

The confrontation between these two men originated in the desire of a number of Englishman to return to their permanent postings overland, through French-held territory, instead of by sea. Some men with connections secured a safe conduct for their party. Accompanying them was a squire named Nicholas Clifford. The company came across a group of French men-at-arms at an inn and they chatted amiably until one Frenchmen, Jean Boucinel, singled out Clifford and claimed that they had an unresolved challenge and now was the perfect time to fight it out. Clifford felt no such urgency, and suggested that the combat be undertaken outside the city of Cherbourg, where he was part of the garrison. But Boucinel was insistent and brushed off every excuse Clifford could come up with. Froissart makes it quite clear that Clifford knew he looked bad, but he held out until Olivier de Clisson, the constable of France, who was nearby, insisted that the challenge take place the next day and arrested the entire company of Englishman to make sure it happened.

The next day the two men armored up—Clifford using borrowed equipment provided by Boucinel—and began the deed with a joust. On the very first pass Clifford's lance caught Boucinel in the throat and killed him. The English party, Clifford in particular, surrounded as they were by Frenchmen, were shocked that the ostensibly friendly deed had gone wrong and were very worried about what might happen next. Boucinel had been a popular man and his lord, also present, was devastated by the death of his favorite. The only thing that happened, however, was that the constable insisted that the English come to dinner, during which he taught them a little lesson. Addressing Nicholas Clifford he said, "I see by your looks, that you are very upset at the death of Jean Boucinel; but I acquit you of it... You have done nothing more than I would have done, as it is better to hurt one's enemy than to be hurt by him. Such are the vicissitudes of arms." An obvious point, perhaps, but there's more to it than the literal words. Once again, it is the French who show a true understanding of the life of arms, in this case showing how one can be gracious despite a heartfelt loss. The episode ends with the Constable providing the English company with an escort to see them safely through to Cherbourg.

The degree of finer feeling attributed here to the French becomes clearer if one postulates an English version of the story. It would be the easiest thing possible to present this as a case of the proud Frenchman, a presumptuous one, who rudely insisted, as Farrington did in Cabaret's version of the deeds at Vannes, that the challenge be fought now and on his own terms. Nicholas Clifford could be the hero of the story. But he is not—he is just another Englishman bumbling through the life of arms.

Chivalric Combat and Practical Warfare

Chivalry is a multifarious term, which as often as not has nothing to do with military practices and customs which originally gave rise to the word. For the past two centuries and more "chivalry" has been a weapon in debates about courtesy and civility in modern life. Even purely military usages tend to imply an ideal standard of behavior that has seldom been achieved. Thus, chivalric combat is a slippery concept. It can be taken as war fought between equals, between gentlemen, a less savage kind of war than that of other eras. Even a cursory investigation of what war in the fourteenth century was like shows that both good men-at-arms and their less respectable retainers were often implicated in the dirtiest practices.

But there were other meanings of the word. Geoffroi de Charny, one of the foremost French knights of the previous generation, discussed chivalry in three works, but did not precisely define it. Yet it is clear that professionalism and courage made the true men-at-arms – even those who were not formally knights. Such men-at-arms took their social duty to fight seriously, overcoming the fear lesser men felt. A chivalrous warrior faced danger head-on and did not back down; that was what distinguished "the chivalry" from ordinary timid men. Likewise Charny emphasized the dignity of the "order of chivalry," which came from the fact that it was the most dangerous way of life practiced by any member of the Christian community.

With this in mind, we can see how a pitched battle or a formal challenge between champions of opposed armies could be rated as the most worthy kind of "chivalric combat." It was a straightforward test of courage and strength and skill. Such combats were a favorite subject for romancers and historians. Structural and symbolic similarities between such combats and trial by combat increased the prestige of face-to-face conflict, in which individuals, companies, and causes could be judged—both by God and by human observers. Among the human observers would of course be other good men-at-arms, whose expert opinions would have a special significance.

But if the pitched battle or the formal challenge was uniquely satisfying, allowing good men-at-arms to justify themselves and establish their worth before the eyes of the world, such chivalrous combat was not the sum total of real warfare. The point of warfare was not to die for your lord or your country, but to overcome and defeat the enemy, who of course was in the wrong. Charny's writings make it clear that the ranking warriors of France used the word "honorable" to indicate not just proper behavior, but wealth, success, and respect derived from rank and capability. It was possible under some circumstances to leave the field of battle and retain one's honor. The entire history of medieval warfare says that it was also possible and sometimes necessary and advantageous to use devious tactics to defeat one's enemy; likewise a wise captain might need to admit that a given battle was lost and leave the field, and live to fight another day. These might be less satisfying ways to fight a war, and make for less satisfying stories in the aftermath. Yet good men-at-arms who knew the risks of real face-to-face combat did not scorn victories won in this way, nor defeats avoided.

The stories collected in *Will a Frenchman Fight?* illustrate the psychological stresses and strains that professional warriors, men with a proud family tradition of excelling in warfare, might have to resolve in order to both win the day and maintain and enhance their reputation.

The Sources

Buckingham's Campaign Begins (Froissart)

BOOK II CHAPTER XLIX.—The duke of Brittany requests succor from the King of England. The earl of Buckingham, youngest son of the late king, is appointed commander of the expedition.

Johnes 1: 602-4; KL 9: 213

You have heard before that when the duke of Brittany left England, King Richard and his uncles promised him aid in the form of men-at-arms and archers, which they performed with ill success; for this was the expedition under the command of Sir John Arundel, who with two hundred men-at-arms were shipwrecked, he himself drowned, with four hundred archers, and from which Sir Hugh Calverley and Sir Thomas Trivet most narrowly escaped. This unfortunate event put an end to the expedition, which was not known to the duke of Brittany. He and his council were exceedingly surprised, and could not conceive what was become of the English; for they were very anxious to profit by their assistance, in the sharp war which was being carried on against the duke by Sir Oliver de

Clisson, Sir Guy de Laval, Sir Oliver du Guesclin, the count de Longueville, the lord de Rochefort, and the French on the frontiers of his duchy.

The duke was advised to send some able men to England, to find out why the reinforcements were not sent as promised, and to hasten them over, for they were in great need of them. The lord de Beaumanoir and Sir Eustace de la Houssaye were entreated by the duke and his nobility to make this journey to England: they answered, they would willingly comply. Letters were given to them by the duke and the nobles of the country; they departed, and embarked at Vannes, with a favorable wind, and arrived at Southampton. They there disembarked, and, having mounted their horses, went to London. It was about Whitsuntide [May 13], in the year of grace 1380.

The arrival of these two lords was soon reported to the king [Richard II] and to his three uncles. The Whitsun feast being arrived, the king went to Windsor to celebrate it, attended by his uncles and great numbers of the barons and knights of England. The two ambassadors went thither also, and were graciously received by the king and the barons, when they presented their letters to his majesty and his uncles. After they had perused them, they knew the great need the duke of Brittany had for assistance, from the earnest entreaties he and the country made for it.

The ambassadors then first heard of the death of Sir John Arundel and his companions, who had perished at sea on their voyage to Brittany. The duke of Lancaster made excuses, saying, it was not owing to any fault of the king or his ministers, but ill fortune at sea, against which none can make headway when God wills it so. The ambassadors, therefore, fully acquitted the king, and greatly lamented the deaths of those knights and squires who had perished. When the feasts of Whitsuntide were over, a parliament was held at Westminster, to which were summoned all the members of the council.

While these things were passing, Sir Guiscard d'Angle, earl of Huntingdon, departed this life in the city of London. He was buried in the church of the Augustinian friars. The king ordered his obsequies to be most honorably performed, and they were attended by a great number of the prelates and barons of England: the bishop of London sang mass. Soon after the parliament was opened, the lord Thomas [earl of Buckingham], youngest son of the late king of England, and many barons, knights, and squires of the realm, were ordered to cross the sea to Calais; and, if God should permit, they were to march through

France, with three thousand men-at-arms and as many archers, so that the lord Thomas might arrive in Brittany, attended by earls, barons, and knights, suitably to the dignity of a king's son. He undertook a bold task to pass through the kingdom of France, which is so extensive and noble, and which has such gallant chivalry and valiant men-at-arms.

When everything relative to this expedition had been discussed and finally arranged, the king of England and his uncles wrote letters to the duke of Brittany and to the nobles of the country, informing them in part of their will, what had been determined on by the parliament, and that for a certainty the earl of Buckingham would this season cross the sea to march to their aid. The king of England showed the ambassadors many honors, and gave them very rich presents, as also did his uncles, when they set out on their departure for Brittany. They presented their letters to the duke, who, having opened and read them, showed them to the states of his country, who were satisfied with their contents. The king of England and his uncles did not delay this expedition, but sent summons to all those who had been selected to attend the earl of Buckingham; the barons to assemble in one place, and the knights in another. They had their wages paid them at Dover for three months, which were to commence as soon as they should land at Calais, for both the men-at-arms and the archers, and their passage over was given to them. They crossed in small parties to Calais, and it was upwards of fifteen days before the whole had there landed.

Those of Boulogne observed these large bodies of men-at-arms continually crossing from Dover to Calais, and informed the whole country and the different garrisons, so that they might not be surprised. When this intelligence was known in the Boulonnois, the Terouennois, and in the county of Guines, all the knights and squires of those countries placed their wealth in different strong towns, to avoid losing it. The governors of Boulogne, Ardres, de la Montoire, d'Esperleck, de Tournehem, de Nordt, de Liques, and of other castles on the frontiers, exerted themselves greatly in strengthening and victualing their garrisons; for they knew that since the English had crossed over with so large a fleet, they would be attacked.

News of this armament was carried to the King of France, who resided at Paris. He sent immediate orders to the lord de Couci, who at that time was at St. Quentin, to provide himself with men-at-arms, and to march to Picardy, to reinforce all the towns, cities, and castles in that province. The lord de Couci duly obeyed the king's orders, and issued his summons at Peronne in the Vermandois, for the immediate assembling of all knights and squires of Artois, Vermandois, and Picardy. The lord de Saimpi was at that time governor of Ardres, and Sir Jean de Bouillé of Boulogne.

The earl of Buckingham arrived at Calais, with his army three days before Magdalen-day, in the month of July 1380.

CHAPTER L.—The earl of Buckingham marches with his army from Calais.

Johnes 604-7 ; KL 9:243

The garrison in Calais rejoiced at the arrival of the earl of Buckingham, for they well knew it would not be long before they began their march. The earl having refreshed himself for two days at Calais, departed on the third, and took the field, following the road towards Marquise. It is proper I should name to you the banners and pennons under the earl's command: first, the earl himself, and the earl of Stafford who had married his niece, a daughter of the lord de Couci, rode with displayed banners; the earl of Devonshire, the lord Despencer, who was constable of the army, the lord Fitzwalter, marshal, the lord Basset, the lord Bourchier, the lord Ferrars, the lord Morley, the lord Darcey, Sir William Windsor, Sir Hugh Calverley, Sir Hugh Hastings, and Sir Hugh de la Sente, advanced with their pennons; lord Thomas Percy, Sir Thomas Trivet, Sir William Clinton, Sir Evan de Fitzwarren, Sir Hugh Tyrrel, the lord Delawarr, Sir Eustace and Sir John de Harbeston, Sir William Farrington, the lord de Braose, Sir William Fabre, Sir John and Sir Nicholas d'Ambreticourt, Sir John Macé, Sir Thomas Camois, Sir Ralph, son to the lord Neville, Sir Henry, bastard of Ferrars, Sir Hugh Broc, Sir Geoffry Worseley, Sir Thomas West, the lord de Saincte More, David Holgrave, Huguelin de Calverley, bastard, Bernard de Coderieres, and several more.

These men-at-arms rode on in handsome array, but did not march farther the day they had left Calais than to Marquise, where they halted to attend to their affairs, and to hold a council on which road they should take to accomplish their expedition; for there were several among them who had never been in France before: in particular, the king's son, and many barons and knights. It was therefore only reasonable, that those who were acquainted with the kingdom of France, and having formerly passed through, and had several engagements in it, should have such weight given to their advice and opinions as redounded to their honor. It is that in former times, when the English invaded France, they had made a regulation for the leaders to swear, in the presence of the king and his council, to observe two things; that to no one, except to themselves, would they reveal the secrets of their councils, their intended march, nor what might be their intentions; and secondly, that they would never agree to any treaty with the enemy without the knowledge and consent of the king and his council.

When these barons, knights, and squires, with their men, had remained for three days at Marquise, and their whole force had joined them from Calais, the captains, having well considered their line of march, departed, and took the road to Ardres. They halted before the castle of Ardres, to show themselves to the garrison within; then the earl of Buckingham created the earl of Devonshire and the lord Morley knights, and these two lords first displayed their banners. The earl of Buckingham created also the following knights: the son of the lord Fitzwalter, Sir Roger Strange, Sir John d'Ypre, Sir John Cole, Sir James Tyrrel, Sir Thomas Ramestone, Sir John Neville, Sir Thomas Roselie. The whole army took up their quarters at Hosque, when the above knights were made. The vanguard then marched to a strong house called Folant, situated upon a river. There was a squire within it of the name of Robert, to whom the house belonged. He was a good man-at-arms, and had well garrisoned it with stores and hardy soldiers, whom he had picked up in the neighborhood, to the amount of forty, who showed every intention to defend themselves well.

These barons and knights, eager to do honor to their new knighthood, surrounded the tower of Folant, and immediately began the attack; but it was well defended by those within. Many a gallant deed was performed; and those in the fort shot well and continually, by which many of the assailants who ventured too near were killed and wounded. There were in the fort some good crossbowmen, whom the governor of St. Omer had sent at the squire's request; for he had imagined the English would pass near his house, and was resolved to defend it the utmost of his power, which he did, for he behaved gallantly. The earl of Devonshire, while he was on the ditch, his banner displayed before him, spoke out bravely, which greatly encouraged his men, saying, "What, my lords! Shall we so much disgrace our new honors as to remain all the day before this pigeon-house?

The strong places and castles in France may well hold out against us, when such a place as this stops us. Advance, advance! Let us prove our knighthoods." Those who heard him took proper notice of what he said, and, sparing themselves less than before, leaped into the ditches, and made for the walls, the archers shooting so briskly that scarcely any dared show themselves on the parapets.

Several were killed and wounded, and the lower court taken and burnt. At length, the whole garrison was made prisoner; but, though they had defended themselves well, none were mortally wounded. Thus was the house of Folant gained, and Robert Folant with his garrison made prisoners by the earl of Devonshire and his men. The whole division took up their quarters on the banks of the river of Hosque, to wait for Sir William Windsor, who commanded the rear-guard. He came thither in the evening. On the morrow, they marched off together, and advanced as far as Esperleck, where they lodged themselves. The governor of St. Omer, finding the enemy so near, doubled his guards, and ordered two thousand men to be in readiness the whole night, that the enemy might not surprise the town. The next day, the English decamped, about six o'clock, and advanced in battle-array before St. Omer. The inhabitants, hearing of their march, armed themselves, according to the orders they had received, and drew up in the marketplace, from whence they went to the gates, towers, and battlements, with a determined resolution to resist, for they had heard that the English would attack the town; but they had no such intentions, for, as it was very strong, they might lose more than they could gain.

The earl of Buckingham, however, who had never before been in France, wished to see St. Omer, because it appeared from its gates, walls, towers, and steeples, to be a handsome place. He drew up and halted his army on a hill about half a league from it, where he remained for three hours. While there, some of the young knights and squires, mounting their coursers, spurred them up to the barriers, and demanded to joust with the knights in the town; but, no answers being made to them, they returned back to the army. The day the earl came before St. Omer, he made more knights; among whom were Sir Ralph Neville, Sir Bartholomew Bourchier, Sir Thomas Camois, Sir Foulke Corbet, Sir Thomas d'Angleere, Sir Ralph Patipas, Sir Lewis St. Aubin, and Sir John Paulet. These new knights, in the first vigor of chivalry, mounted their horses, and galloped up to the gates, calling on the knights within to joust with them; but they experienced the same neglect as the others had done.

When the army saw that the French lords in St. Omer made no attempt to come out to meet them, they continued their march, and came that, day to Esquilles, between St. Omer and Terouenne, where they took up their quarters for the night. On the morrow, they departed, and made for Terouenne. The French garrisons in the counties of Boulogne, Artois, and Guines, having observed the dispositions of the English, that they continued their march without stopping at any place, mutually informed each other of their intentions to follow them, since much might be gained by it: they therefore assembled, under the pennons of the lord de Fransures and the lord de Saimpi, to the number of more than two hundred lances. They pursued the English army; but, though they kept close to them, the English marched in such compact order, they were not put into the least disorder, and their enemies could not attack them, without the risk of suffering a total defeat. These French knights and squires, however, at times fell upon the English foragers, so that they dared not forage but in large companies.

The English passed Terouenne without attempting anything, for the lords de Saimpi and de Fransures were inside. They marched on towards Bethune, where they halted for a day; and I will tell you the reason. You have before heard how King Richard, by the advice of his uncles and council, had sent Sir Simon Burley to Germany, to the emperor, to demand his sister in marriage. This knight so well managed the business that the emperor, by advice of his council and the great lords of his court, complied with the request, but he had sent, with Sir Simon Burley, the duke of Saxony, first to Luxembourg and then to England, to observe that kingdom, in order that his sister might have a just account of it, so that, if agreeable, the marriage might be concluded.

The cardinal of Ravenna was at that time in England, and, being a supporter of Pope Urban, was converting the English to the same way of thinking: he was also waiting the arrival of the above-mentioned duke. At the entreaties of the emperor and the duke of Brabant, he and all his company obtained liberty to pass through France to Calais. They therefore travelled by way of Tournay, Lille, and Bethune, from whence they came to visit the earl of Buckingham and his barons, who received the duke of Saxony and his suite most honorably. The Germans continued their journey through Aire and St. Omer, and from thence to Calais.

The earl of Buckingham marched his army before Liques, and encamped that same day at Bouhain les Bouissieres; but they were constantly followed by the lords de Saimpi and de Fransures with their forces. In the morning, they advanced nearer to Bethune. There were in that town a numerous garrison of men-at-arms, knights and squires, whom the lord de Couci had sent; such as the lord de Hangest, Sir John and Sir Tristan de Roye, Sir Geoffroi de Charny, Sir Guy de Harcourt, and many more. The army passed by Bethune without making any attempt to attack it, and lay at Doncheres.

In the evening the lords de Saimpi and de Fransures entered Bethune, and the next day went to Arras, where they met the lord de Couci, who received them very politely, inquiring news from them, and which road the English had taken. They replied that they had lodged the preceding night at Doncheres; that they marched with very great prudence, for they constantly kept in close order. "It is then clear," answered the lord de Couci, "that they wish for battle; which they shall have, if the king our lord will trust us, before they have finished their march." The earl marched by Arras, in order of battle, continuing his route without doing anything: he took up his quarters at Anet, on the morrow at Miraumont and the next day at Clery-on-the-Somme.

The lord de Couci, who resided at Arras, on hearing they had taken this road, sent the lord Hangest to Braye-sur-Somme, and with him thirty lances, knights and squires: he ordered Sir James de Verchin, seneschal of Hainault, the lord de Hamireth, Sir Jean de Roye, and several others to go to Peronne: he himself went to St. Quentin. He sent the lord de Clery, with others, into the Vermandois; for he was anxious that no loss should be suffered through any negligence on his part.

CHAPTER LI.—The lord de Brimeu, his sons, and his men are taken prisoners by the English. The garrison of Peronne are driven back into that town.

Johnes 1: 607-8; KL 9: 252

The night the English had quartered themselves at Clery-on-the-Somme, some knights of the army, such as Sir Thomas Trivet, Sir William Clinton, Sir Evan Fitzwarren, at the instigation of the lord Delawarr, who was well acquainted with the whole country, and knew that the lord de Coney was with a large body of men-at-arms in the town of Arras, resolved to march from the army at early dawn with the foragers, to see if they should meet with any adventure worth attending to; for they wished to perform some deed of arms. As they had planned, so did they execute; and about thirty lances set out after the foragers, in search of adventures.

This same day, the lord de Couci had left Arras with a large body of men, and had taken the road to St. Quentin. When they were on their march, the lord de Brimeu, his sons, with about thirty spears, left the army of the lord de Couci, anxious to perform some gallant act. These two bodies of English and French, meeting in the plains, saw a combat was inevitable: they therefore struck spurs into their horses, and galloped towards each other, shouting their war cries. On the first shock, several were unhorsed, killed and wounded on both sides. Many handsome deeds were done: they dismounted, and began to thrust with their spears, each party behaving bravely. This mode of combat continued about an hour, and no one could say to whom would be the victory, but in the end the English won the field. Sir Thomas Trivet made prisoners of the lord de Brimeu, and his two sons, Jean and Lewis, and sixteen men-at-arms: the rest saved themselves: and the English returned to their army with their prisoners. They remained some little time in the neighborhood of Peronne, having heard from their prisoners that the lord de Couci was in that town with upwards of a thousand lances, and they did not know if he wished to offer them battle.

This day the lord Delawarr, with Fierabras his bastard-brother, Sir Evan Fitzwarren and several others, leaving the army, hastened to Mont St. Quentin, where they posted themselves in ambuscade; for they had learnt that the seneschal of Hainault was in Peronne with a strong body of men-at-arms, and they knew him to be so self-sufficient that he would not fail to sally out, which in truth he did. The vanguard ordered ten men-at-arms to march to Peronne; among whom were Thierry de Soumain, Fierabras, Sir Hugh Calverley and Hopoquin Hay, mounted on their chargers. They galloped up to the barriers, where there were at least fifty spears with the seneschal of Hainault; who, thinking to catch these gallopers, ordered the barriers to be thrown open, and immediately began a pursuit after them, as they retreated towards their ambuscade.

When those who had placed themselves in ambush saw the French pursuing their men, they revealed themselves; but it was somewhat too soon, for when the seneschal perceived this large body so well mounted, he sounded a retreat, and the horses then knew the effect of spurs: very opportunely did these lords find the barriers open. They were, however, so closely followed, that Sir Richard de Marqueillies, Sir Louis de Vertaing, Honard de la Honarderie, Vital de St. Hilaire, with ten other men-at-arms, remained prisoners withthe English; the others escaped. When the English learnt that the seneschal of Hainault, the lord de Hamireth, the lord de Clery, with twenty other knights, had escaped, they cried out, " God! What a fortunate event would it have been, if we had taken them, for they would have paid us forty thousand francs." They returned to the army, and nothing more was done that day.

The army remained for three days at Clery-sur-Somme, and in that neighborhood. On the fourth, they marched away, and came to the abbey of Vaucelle, three leagues from Cambray, and the next day nearer St. Quentin. This day, about thirty spears attached to the duke of Burgundy had set out from Arras for St. Quentin. Sir Thomas Trivet, Sir Evan Fitzwarren, the lord Delawarr, and several others who had been from the vanguard with the foragers, as they were about to decide on their quarters, fell in with the Burgundians, and a battle ensued: but it did not last long, for the Burgundians were soon dispersed, one here, another there, and all tried to save themselves as well as they could. Sir Jean de Mornay, however, stood his ground in good order, with his pennon before him, and fought valiantly, but at last was taken, and ten men of his company. The English then marched to Foursons, two leagues from Amiens, where the vanguard quartered itself.

CHAPTER LII.—The English burn and despoil Champagne. —They meet with various adventures on their march, and take many prisoners.

Johnes 1: 608-10; KL 9: 256

On the ensuing morning, when the earl of Buckingham and his army had heard mass, they began their march towards St. Quentin; in which town there were numbers of men-at-arms, but they did not sally forth. Some of the light troops galloped up to the barriers, and soon returned; for the army continued its march, without halting, until it arrived at Origny St. Benoiste and the adjacent villages. In the town of Origny, there was a handsome nunnery, the abbess of which at that time happened to be aunt-in-law to the lord Delawarr, at whose entreaty the nunnery and the whole town were spared from being burnt and pillaged: the earl was lodged in the abbey. That evening and the following morning, there were many skirmishes at Ribemont, which was hard by, when several were slain and wounded on each side. In the morning, the army dislodged from Origny, came to Crecy, and passed Vaux below Laon, fixing their quarters at Sissonne. The next day, they crossed the river Aisne at Pont à Vaire, and came to Hermonville and Coumissy, four leagues from Rheims, without meeting with any forage on their march.

Everything had been driven or carried into the towns and strong places, the king of France having abandoned to his own men-at-arms whatever they could find in the open country: the English, therefore, suffered great distress for lack of food. They determined to send a herald to Rheims, to open a treaty with the inhabitants, for them to send provisions to the army, such as cattle, bread and wine. The inhabitants refused to enter into any negotiation, and, in their reply, said, they must make the best of it. This answer so much enraged them that, in one week, the light troops burnt upwards of sixty villages dependent on Rheims. The English heard that the people of Rheims had secured six thousand sheep in the ditches of the town, thinking them safe there: the vanguard advanced thither, and made their men descend into the ditches and drive out the sheep, without anyone daring to issue from the town to prevent them, or even appearing on the bulwarks; for the archers, being posted on the banks of the ditch, shot so sharply that no one ventured to show himself: the English gained several thousand head of sheep. They sent to inform the townsmen, they would burn all the corn in the fields, unless they ransomed it by sending them bread and wine. The inhabitants were frightened by this threat, and sent the army from ten to sixteen loads of bread and wine: by this means, the corn and oats were saved from being burnt. The English marched by Rheims in order of battle to Beaumont-sur-Vesle, for they had crossed the river below Rheims. On their departure from Beaumont, the English rode along the river Marne, to seek a passage, and came to Conde sur Marne, where they found the bridge broken down; but, as the supporters still remained, they looked for planks and beams, with which they rebuilt the bridge, crossed the river, and quartered themselves in the villages above Marne; and on the ensuing day, they came before the town of Vertus, when there was a grand skirmish in front of the castle, in which many were wounded.

The earl of Buckingham was lodged in the abbey. During the night, the town was burnt, except the abbey, which, because the earl was lodging in it, was saved; otherwise it would infallibly have suffered the same fate, for the townsmen had retreated into the castle, and would not ransom it. The army marched off the following day, and passed by the castle of Moymer, which is the inheritance of the lord de Chastillon. The skirmishers advanced to the barriers, and then passed on and took up their quarters for the night at Pelange, making for the city of Troyes, and the next day at Plancy sur Aube. The lord de Chateauneuf and Jean de Chateauneuf his brother, with Remond St. Marsin, Gascons, and some English, about forty spears in the whole, rode from the army to seek adventures, but met with none, which vexed them very much. On their return, they saw in the plain a body of men-at-arms riding towards Troyes: it was the lord de Hangest and his men: the English and Gascons immediately spurred their horses to come up with them. The lord de Hangest had well observed them, and, doubting they were in greater numbers than they appeared, said to his men, "Make for Plancy and save yourselves; for these English have discovered us, and their main army is not far off: let us put ourselves in safety in the castle of Plancy." They rode in that direction, and the English after them.

There was a valiant man-at-arms from Hainault in the troop of the lord Delawarr, called Peter Berton, who fixing his lance in its rest, and being well mounted, came up with the lord de Hangest, who was flying before him, and gave him such a blow on the back with his lance that he almost drove him out of the saddle; but the lord de Hangest neither lost his seat nor stirrups, though Peter Berton kept the iron hard at his back; and in this manner they arrived at Plancy. Straight at the entrance of the castle the lord de Hangest leaped from his horse, and got into the ditch. Those within it were anxious to save him, and ran to the barriers, where there was a grand skirmish; for the garrison kept shooting briskly, being very good crossbowmen; and several valiant deeds were done on each side. With great difficulty the lord de Hangest was saved. He fought gallantly on entering the castle; for reinforcements from the vanguard were continually arriving. The lord Delawarr, Sir Thomas Trivet, Sir Hugh Calverley, came thither, and the conflict was great: there were upwards of thirty of the French killed and wounded, and the lower court of the castle burnt. The castle itself was warmly attacked on all sides, but well defended: the mills of Plancy were burnt and destroyed. The whole army then retired, passed the river Aube at Pont a l'Ange, and marched towards Valant-sur-Seine. The lord de Hangest had a very narrow escape.

This same day the captains of the vanguard, Sir Thomas Trivet, Sir Hugh Calverley, the lord Delawarr, the bastard his brother, Peter Berton and many others, made an excursion from the army, and met Sir Jean de Roye, with about twenty spears of the duke of Burgundy who were going to Troyes. The English, on seeing them, spurred their horses; for the French were making off, as not in sufficient numbers to wait for them. The greater part did escape; and Sir Jean de Roye, with others, got within the barriers of Troyes, which at the time chanced to be open. On their return, they captured four of his men who could not save themselves, among whom was a squire to the duke of Burgundy, called Guion Goufer, an expert man-at-arms. His horse was much heated, so that he had dismounted, and, having placed himself against a walnut tree, fought valiantly against two Englishmen, who pressed him hard, crying out to him in English to surrender; but he did not understand them. Fierabras, on his return from the pursuit, arriving at the spot, said to the squire in French, "Surrender." On hearing this, he replied, "Are you a gentleman?" The bastard rejoined he was. "I then surrender myself to you," presenting him his sword and gauntlet; for which the English would have killed him when he was in the bastard's hands, and they told him he was not very courteous to deprive them of their prisoner, but the bastard was stronger than they. Nevertheless this affair was, in the evening, brought before the marshals, who, having well considered it, determined he should remain to the bastard, who that evening ransomed him, taking his word for the payment, and sent him on the morrow to Troyes. The whole army was quartered at Valant sur Seine, and the next day after crossing the Seine at a ford, came to a village one league from Troyes, called Bernard-Saint-Simple, where the lords and captains held many councils.

The Confrontation at Troyes (Froissart)

CHAPTER LIII. The English come before Troyes.—A skirmish at one of the gates.—They take a fort which the duke of Burgundy had erected on the outside.—King Charles conspires with the inhabitants of Nantes.

Johnes 1: 610-3; KL 9: 263

The duke of Burgundy was in the city of Troyes, and had fixed on that place for the rendezvous of his forces. His intentions were to fight the English between the rivers Seine and Yonne; and the barons, knights and squires of France did not wish for anything better; but Charles of France, doubtful of the fortune of the war, would not give his permission so to do. He recollected too well the great losses his nobles had formerly suffered from the victories of the English, and would never allow them to fight unless the advantages were very considerable on their side. There were with the duke of Burgundy, in Troyes, the duke of Bourbon, the duke of Bar, the count d'Eu, the lord de Couci, Sir Jean de Vienne, admiral of France, the lord de Vienne, and de Sainte Croix, Sir James de Vienne, Sir Walter de Vienne, the lord de la Trémouille, the lord de Vergy, the lord de Rougemont, the lord de Hambue, the seneschal of Hainault, the lord de Saimpi, the baron des Barres, the lord de Roye, the viscount d'Assi, Sir William bastard de Langres, with upwards of two thousand knights and squires. I was informed that the lord de la Trémouille was sent by the duke and the other lords to Paris, to entreat the king to allow them to fight; and he was not returned at the time the English came before Troyes. The lords of France, doubting the English would not pass by without coming to look at them, had erected, about a bow-shot from the gates of Troyes, a large redoubt of great beams of timber, which might hold about a thousand men-at-arms: it was made of good strong wood, and well built.

All the captains of the English army were summoned to a council, to consider in what manner they should act the ensuing day. It was resolved, that all the lords and knights should march, fully armed with their banners and pennons displayed, before Troyes: they were to draw up in the plain, and to send their heralds to offer battle to those in the town. They armed themselves, therefore, on the morrow, and, being formed in three battalions, advanced into the plain before Troyes, where they halted. The two heralds, Gloucester and Aquitaine, were called, when the earl of Buckingham said to them: "You will go to Troyes, and tell the lords within the city that we are come from England in search of deeds of arms: wherever we think they can be found, there we shall demand them: and, because we know that a part of the lilies and chivalry of France repose in the town of Troyes, we have purposely come this road. If they wish to say anything to us, they will find us in the open plain in the form and manner in which you shall leave us, and in such a way as we ought to meet our enemies." The heralds replied, "My lord, we shall obey your commands."

They then set off, and rode to Troyes. The entrance of the redoubt was opened to them, where they stopped; for they could not get to the gate of the town from the numbers of men-at-arms and cross-bowmen issuing forth, and drawing up before this redoubt. The two heralds wore the emblazoned arms of the earl of Buckingham: they were asked by the lords, what they wanted: they answered, they wished, if it were possible, to speak with the duke of Burgundy.

During the time the heralds were endeavoring to deliver their message to the duke of Burgundy, the English were arranging their battalions; for they looked on a battle as certain. All who were desirous of knighthood were called: first Sir Thomas Trivet, with his banner rolled up, came to the earl of Buckingham, and said: "My lord, if you please, I will this day display my banner; for, thanks to God, I have a sufficient revenue to support the state which a banner requires."

"It is highly pleasing to us," replied the earl: then, taking the banner by the staff, he gave it back into his hands, saying, "Sir Thomas, God grant you may show your valor here, and everywhere else." Sir Thomas took his banner, and, having displayed it, gave it to one of his squires in whom he had great confidence, and went to the vanguard; for he was there stationed by orders from the lord Latimer and the lord Fitzwalter, captain and constable. The earl then created the following knights: Sir Peter Berton, Sir John and Sir Thomas Paulet, Sir John Stingulie, Sir Thomas Dortingues, Sir John Vassecoq, Sir John Brasie, Sir John Buraine, Sir Henry Vernier, Sir John Colville, sir William Everat, Sir Nicholas Stingulie and Sir Hugh de Lunit. They advanced to the van battalion, in order to have their share of the first blows.

A very gallant squire from the country of Savoy was then called, who had before been requested to be made a knight at St. Omer and at Ardres: his name was Ralph de Gruyeres, son to the count de Gruyeres: when the earl said to him, "We shall have an engagement today, if it please God, and I will make you a knight,"—the squire excused himself, saying, "God give you all the good and honor you wish me; but I will never be a knight until my natural lord, the count of Savoy, shall confer it upon me in battle." He was not pressed farther on this subject.

It was a pleasure to observe the order of battle in which the English were drawn up; and the French were busy in strengthening their forts, for they concluded that at least there would be some skirmishes, and that such warriors as the English would not depart without a nearer examination of them. The French formed themselves handsomely: and the duke of Burgundy was abroad, with his battle-axe in his hand, armed from head to foot: he passed in review all the knights and squires as they marched to the fort; and the crowd was so great, there was not any passing, nor could the heralds arrive as far as the duke to deliver the message with which they had been charged.

To the words which the earl of Buckingham had delivered to the heralds Gloucester and Aquitaine, others were added; for, on the evening when the lords had held their council, they told the heralds: "You will carry this message, and tell the duke of Burgundy, that the duke and country of Brittany in conjunction have sent to the king of England, for support and aid against certain knights and barons of Brittany in rebellion against the said duke, whom they refuse to obey as their lord, as the better disposed part of the country do, but carry on war, in which they are supported by the king of France. On this account, the king of England is resolved to assist the duke and the country, and has ordered his fair uncle the earl of Buckingham, with a large body of men-at-arms, to march to Brittany for this purpose. They landed at Calais, and, having marched through the kingdom of France, are now so much in the heart of it as to be arrived before the city of Troyes, wherein they know are great numbers of the nobility: in particular, the duke of Burgundy, son of the late king of France and brother to the king now on the throne: therefore, the lord Thomas of Buckingham, son to the late king of England, demands a battle." The heralds requested to have this put down in writing, which they were promised to have on the morrow; but, when they again asked for it, they had changed their opinions, and no letters were given: but they were told to go, and say what they had heard, as they were of sufficient credit; "and, if they choose, they will believe you." The heralds could not approach near enough to the duke to deliver their message, nor obtain any answer.

The young English knights had already begun to skirmish, which had troubled everything, and some French knights and men-at-arms said to the heralds, "Gentlemen, you are in a hazardous situation, for the common people of this town are very wicked." This hint made them return without doing anything. We will now relate the beginning of the skirmish. In the first place, there was an English squire, a native of the bishopric of Lincoln, who was an excellent man-at-arms, and there gave proofs of his courage. I do not know if he had made any vow; but with his lance in its rest, his shield on his neck, he spurred his horse, and, riding full gallop down the causeway, he made him leap over the bars of the barriers, and came to the gate where the duke was, surrounded by the French nobility, who looked on this enterprise with amazement. The squire intended returning; but he was prevented by his horse receiving a blow from a spear, which felled him and killed the squire. It much angered the duke that he had not been made prisoner.

Instantly the battalions of the earl of Buckingham advanced on foot, to the attack of the men-at-arms in the wooden redoubt, which had been formed of shutters, doors and tables, and was not, to say the truth, fit to hold out against such men-at-arms as the English. When the duke of Burgundy saw them advance in such numbers, and with so much spirit, that the lords, barons and knights in this fort were not strong enough to withstand them, he directly ordered them to retreat into the town, excepting the crossbowmen. They retired, by little and little, to the gate; and, as they were entering it, the Genoese crossbowmen shot and wounded the English. There was a good and sharp skirmish: the redoubt was soon conquered, but it did not long remain to the English. All sorts of people came in great strength to the gates; and, as they passed, they drew up on the causeways. The duke of Lorraine was there handsomely disposed; as were the lord de Couci, the duke of Bourbon, and others. Between this gate and the bars, many valorous deeds were done, and of course numbers were slain, wounded and taken. The English, seeing the French retreat, retreated also in excellent order, and formed themselves on the plain, in battle-array, for upwards of two hours; when, towards evening, they retired to their quarters.

The next day, the army marched to Maillerois-le-Vicomte, near Sens in Burgundy, where they halted for two days, to refresh themselves and to gather provision from the low countries, of which they were in the greatest need.

You have heard how the English marched through France, and thus took the road to Brittany. They publicly declared the duke and country of Brittany had sent for them, and that they had not any pretense for waging war in the name of the king of England their lord, but that they were then in the pay of the duke of Brittany. King Charles was at the time fully informed of all these matters, and, like a wise and prudent man as he was, examined well all the perils and incidents which might arise from them. He considered, that if Brittany joined these English against him, the fortune of war would be more doubtful; and, as he was on bad terms with the duke, if the principal towns were to open their gates to his enemies, it would turn out very much to his prejudice. He therefore sent, secretly, letters sealed, but written in the most gracious manner, to the inhabitants of Nantes (which is the key to all the other towns in Brittany), to request they would consider that the English, who were marching through his kingdom, boasted they were sent for by them, and declared themselves to be their soldiers; and that if they had actually engaged them, and were to persevere in this evil act, they would incur the malediction of their holy father the pope, according to the sentence he had passed, as well as the penalty of two hundred thousand florins, which he could legally demand from them, and which they had bound themselves to pay, according to treaties sealed which had formerly passed between them, and of which he had copies, as they must know: that he had ever been their friend, and had assisted them in all their necessities; and that by persisting in this matter they would be very much to blame, for they had not any well-grounded complaint against him to induce them to enter so warmly into the war and to receive his enemies. He therefore recommended them maturely to reconsider this; and, if they had been wickedly or ill advised, he would frankly forgive it, provided they did not open their gates to his enemies the English, and would maintain them in all just rights and privileges, and even renew them, should there be occasion.

When these letters and offers from the king of France had been read by the men of Nantes and considered, the principal persons among them said, the king of France was in the right, and he had cause for remonstrating with them as he had done; that in truth they had sworn and sealed never to be enemies themselves to the kingdom of France, nor to give any assistance to its enemies. They began, therefore, to be on their guard, and sent privately to the king of France not to be uneasy on this head, as they would never aid or succor the English in their attempts to injure the kingdom of France by force, nor would their town afford them any assistance; for they were determined, if there should be any necessity, to claim the help of the king, and that to his army alone would they open their gates, and to none else. The king of France, having received their messenger, put confidence in their declarations, for Nantes was always attached to the French interest: of all this, however, the duke, who resided at Vannes, was ignorant: he thought, nevertheless, that the inhabitants of Nantes would remain steady to him, and that they would open their gates to the English when they should come thither.

We will now return to the English who were quartered near to Sens in Burgundy; in which city the duke of Bar, the lord de Couci, the lord de Saimpi, the lord de Fransures, were in garrison with their troops.

Deeds of Arms at Toury and Marchenoir (Froissart)

CHAPTER LIV.—The English overrun the countries of Gatinois and Beauce.—A French squire demands to joust with an English squire: they both behave very gallantly.

Johnes 1: 613-5; KL 9: 274

When the earl of Buckingham and his army had reposed themselves at Maillerois-le-Vicomte, they determined to advance into the Gatinois: they crossed, in consequence, the river Yonne, and their light troops went even to the suburbs of Sens. The next day they quartered themselves at St. Jean de Nemours and thereabouts, and afterwards at Beaune in Gatinois, where they remained three days, on account of its fertile and rich country. There they held a council, whether to follow the road into the plains of Beauce, or keep to the course of the river Loire: they resolved on the first, and marched towards Toury in Beauce. In this castle were the lord de Saimpi, Sir Oliver de Mauny, Sir Guy le Baveux, and numbers of men-at-arms. There were besides, at Geneville in Beauce, the lord de Volainnes, le Barrois des Barres, with others to the amount of three hundred spears; and in all the castles and fortresses of Beauce were posted men-at-arms to defend the country.

Those of the vanguard skirmished with the garrison of Toury, when there were some slain on both sides. The earl of Buckingham and his whole army were quartered at Toury in Beauce, and in the environs, where they found plenty of provisions. During the skirmish at Toury, a squire from Beauce, a gentleman of tried courage, who had advanced himself by his own merit, without any assistance from others, came to the barriers, and cried out to the English, "Is there among you any gentleman who for love of his lady is willing to try with me some feat of arms? If there should be any such, here I am, quite ready to sally forth completely armed and mounted, to joust three blows with the lance, to give three blows with the battle-axe, and three strokes with the dagger. Now look, you English, if there be none among you in love."

This squire's name was Gauvain Micaille. His proposal and request was soon spread among the English, when a squire, a brave companion and a good jouster called Joachim Cator, stepped forth and said, "I will deliver him from his vow: let him make haste and come out of the castle." Upon this, the lord Fitzwalter, marshal of the army, went up to the barriers, and said to Sir Guy le Baveux, "Let your squire come forth: he has found one who will cheerfully deliver him; and we will afford him every security."

Gauvain Micaille was much rejoiced on hearing these words. He immediately armed himself, in which the lords assisted, in the putting on the different pieces, and mounted him on a horse, which they gave to him. Attended by two others, he came out of the castle; and his valets carried three lances, three battle-axes, and three daggers. And you should know that he was much stared at by the English when he came out, and they thought this enterprise a great bravado, for they did not believe any Frenchman would dare to fight body to body. There were besides to be three strokes with a sword, and with all other sorts of arms. Gauvain had had three brought with him for fear any should break.

The earl of Buckingham, hearing of this combat, said he would see it, and mounted his horse, attended by the earls of Stafford and Devonshire. On this account, the assault on Toury ceased. The Englishman who was going to joust was brought forward, completely armed and mounted on a good horse. When they had taken their stations, they gave to each of them a spear, and the joust began; but neither of them struck the other, from the mettlesomeness of their horses. They hit on the second onset, but it was by darting their spears; on which the earl of Buckingham cried out, "Hola ho! it is now late." He then said to the constable, "Put an end to it, for they have done enough this day: we will make them finish it when we have more leisure than we have at this moment, and take great care that as much attention is paid to the French squire as to our own; and order someone to tell those in the castle not to be uneasy about him, for we shall carry him with us to complete his enterprise, but not as a prisoner; and that when he shall have been delivered, if he escapes with his life, we will send him back in all safety."

These orders of the earl were obeyed by the marshal, who said to the French squire, "You shall accompany us without any danger, and when it shall be agreeable to my lord you will be delivered." Gauvain replied, "God help me!" A herald was sent to the castle, to repeat to the governor the words you have heard.

The following day, they marched towards Geneville in Beauce, always in expectation of having an engagement with the enemy; for they well knew they were followed and watched by the French, in greater numbers than themselves. It is true, that the French dukes, counts, barons, knights, and squires, eagerly wished for a battle, and said among themselves, that it was very blamable and foolish not to permit them to engage, and allow the enemy to slip through their hands. But, when it was mentioned to the king, he replied, "Let them alone: they will destroy themselves." The English continued their march, with the intent to enter Brittany.

You heard before, that there were three hundred spears in Geneville, so the whole army passed by it. There was indeed at the barriers some little skirmishing, which did not last long, as it was a waste of time. Outside Geneville a handsome mill was destroyed. The earl came to Yterville, and dismounted at the house of the Templars. The vanguard went forwards to Puiset, where they heard that sixty companions had posted themselves in a large tower: they marched to the attack, for it was situated in the open plain without any bulwarks. The assault was sharp, but did not last long, for the archers shot so briskly that scarcely any one dared to appear on the battlements: the tower was taken, and those within slain or made prisoners. The English then set fire to it, and marched on, for they were in the utmost distress for water. From thence they went to Ermoyon, where they quartered themselves, and then to the forest of Marchenoir. In this forest there is a monastery of monks, of the Cistercian order, which is called the Cistercian Abbey, and has several handsome and noble edifices, where formerly a most renowned and noble knight, the count de Blois, received great edification, and bequeathed to it large revenues; but the wars had greatly diminished them. The earl of Buckingham lodged in this abbey, and heard mass there on the feast of Our Lady in September. It was there ordered, that Gauvain Micaille and Joachim Cator should on the morrow complete their enterprise. That day the English came to Marchenoir: the governor was a knight of that country, called Sir William de St. Martin, a prudent and valiant man-at-arms. The English, after having reconnoitered the castle, retired to their quarters. In another part, the lord Fitzwalter came before the castle of Verbi, not to attack it, but to speak with the governor at the barriers, with whom he was well acquainted, since they had been together formerly in Prussia. The lord Fitzwalter made himself known to the lord de Verbi, and entreated him, out of courtesy, to send him some wine, and in return he would prevent his estate from being burnt or spoiled. The lord de Verbi sent him a large quantity, and thirty great loaves with it; for which the lord Fitzwalter was very thankful, and kept his promise.

On the day of the feast of Our Lady, Gauvain Micaille and Joachim Cator were armed, and mounted to finish their engagement. They met each other roughly with spears, and the French squire jousted much to the satisfaction of the earl: but the Englishman kept his spear too low, and at last struck it into the thigh of the Frenchman. The earl of Buckingham as well as the other lords were much enraged at this, and said it was jousting dishonorably; but he [Joachim] excused himself, by declaring it was solely owing to the restiveness of his horse. Then they gave the three thrusts with the sword; and the earl declared they had done enough, and would not have it longer continued, for he perceived that the French squire bled exceedingly: the other lords were of the same opinion. Gauvain Micaille was therefore disarmed and his wound dressed. The earl sent him one hundred francs by a herald, with leave to return to his own garrison in safety, adding that he had acquitted himself much to his satisfaction. Gauvain Micaille went back to the lords of France: and the English departed from Marchenoir, taking the road to Vendôme; but before they arrived there, they quartered themselves in the forest of Coulombiers.

CHAPTER LV.—King Charles of France is taken ill.—His last words on his deathbed.

Johnes 1; 615-6; KL 9: 282

You have heard what secret intrigues the king of France was carrying on with the principal towns in Brittany, to prevent them from admitting the English, threatening that those who should do so that they should never be forgiven. The inhabitants of Nantes sent him word not to be alarmed; for they would never consent to admit them, whatever treaties had been entered into with their lord: but they were desirous, if the English should approach, that some men-at-arms might be sent, to defend the town and the inhabitants against their enemies.

The king of France was well inclined to this, and charged his council to see it executed. The mainspring of all these treaties was Sir Jean de Bueil, on the part of the duke of Anjou, who resided at Angers. The duke of Burgundy was quartered in the city of Mans, and in that country. Other lords, such as the duke of Bourbon, the count de Bar, the lord de Couci, the count d'Eu, the duke of Lorraine, were in the neighboring castles and forts, with a force of upwards of six thousand men-at-arms: they said among themselves, that whether the king willed it or not, they would combat the English before they crossed the river Sarthe, which divides Maine from Anjou.

The king of France was at this moment seized with an illness, which much disheartened all who loved him; for, as no remedy could be found for it, they foresaw that in a very short time he must depart this life: indeed, he himself knew this, as well as his surgeons and physicians. The reports were firmly believed, that the king of Navarre, during the time he resided in Normandy, had attempted to poison him, and that the king was so much infected by the venom that the hairs of his head and the nails of his hands and feet fell off, and he became as dry as a stick, for which they could not discover any remedy. His uncle, the emperor, hearing of his illness, sent to him his own physician, the most able man of that time, and of the greatest learning then known in the world, as his works indeed show: he was called a second Aristotle, but his name was George of Prague. When this great doctor came to visit the king, who at that time was duke of Normandy, he recognized his disorder, and declared, that having been poisoned, he was in danger of dying: however, he performed the greatest cure known, by so weakening the force of the poison that he caused him to regain his former strength.

This poison oozed out in small quantities from an issue in his arm. On the departure of the doctor, for they could not detain him, he prescribed a medicine that was to be made use of constantly. He told the king and his attendants that whenever this issue should dry up, he would infallibly die: but that he would have fifteen days or more to settle his affairs, and attend to his soul.

The king of France well remembered these words, and had had this issue for twenty-two years, which at times alarmed him much. Those in whom he put great confidence, in regard to his health, were able physicians, who comforted him, and kept up his spirits, by saying that, with the excellent medicines they had, they would make him live long in joy and happiness, so that he had great faith in them. The king had, besides other disorders that afflicted him much, such as the toothache: from this he suffered the greatest torment; and his majesty knew, from all these symptoms, he could not live very long; but the greatest comfort, towards the end of his days, was in God for having given him three fine children, two sons and a daughter, Charles, Louis, and Catherine.

When this issue began to cease running, the fears of death came upon him: he therefore, like a wise and prudent man, began to look to his affairs. He sent for his three brothers, the duke of Berry, the duke of Burgundy, and the duke of Bourbon, without notifying his next brother, the duke of Anjou, whom he did not send for, because he knew him to be very avaricious. When they were arrived, he said to them: "My dear brothers, I feel I have not long to live: I therefore recommend to your charge my son Charles, to take that care of him as good uncles ought to do for their nephew, by which you will loyally acquit yourselves. Have him crowned king as soon as you possibly can after my decease, and advise him justly in all his affairs. My whole confidence rests in you: the child is young, and, being of an unsteady temper, will want to be well managed and properly instructed in sound learning. Teach him, or have him taught, every point relative to royalty, and the manner in which he should conduct himself according to the situation he may be in. Marry him to such a princess of high birth that the kingdom may gain by it. I have had with me for a considerable time a learned astronomer, who has predicted that in his youth he will have much to do, and escape from great perils and dangers. Having thought much on these expressions, I have considered that the events alluded to must have their origin in Flanders; for, thanks to God, the affairs of my kingdom are in a very good condition. The duke of Brittany is very deceitful and forward, and has always had more of English than French courage; for which reason, you must keep the nobles and principal towns of that country in good affection to you, in order to traverse his designs. I have every cause to praise the Bretons, for they have served me faithfully in the defense of my kingdom against its enemies. You will make the lord de Clisson constable: everything considered, I know no one so proper for that office. Seek out, in Germany, an alliance for my son, that our connections there may be strengthened. You have heard our adversary is about to marry from thence, to increase his allies. The poor people of my realm are much harassed and tormented by taxes and subsidies: take them off as speedily as you can, for they are things which, notwithstanding I proposed them, weigh very heavy on my mind: but the great undertakings we have had to maintain in every part of the kingdom forced me to submit to them." Many more kind words did King Charles utter, but I have not thought it necessary to cite them all. The king explained why the duke of Anjou was absent; for he suspected him much, knowing him to be of an ambitious temper. Notwithstanding the king of France did not permit him to attend his deathbed, nor to have any part in the government of France, this duke did not keep at a very great distance: he had besides messengers continually going between Paris and Angers, who brought him exact accounts of the state of his brother's health. He had also some about the king's person, who informed him secretly what daily passed; and the last day, when the king of France departed this life, he was at Paris, and so near to the king's chamber that he heard all the discourse I have just related. But we will now follow the English in their march to Brittany.

CHAPTER LVI.—The lord de Hangest is nearly taken by the English.—The lord de Mauvoisin remains their prisoner.—The English cross the river Sarthe in disorder.

Johnes 1: 616-7 ; KL 9: 286

When the earl of Buckingham quitted the forest of Marchenoir with his army, he took the road towards Vendôme and the forest of Coulombiers. Sir Thomas Trivet and Sir William Clinton were somewhat advanced, with forty spears, and by accident met the lord de Hangest, who was returning from Vendôme, accompanied by thirty lances. The English soon saw they were French, and eagerly galloped towards them. The French, who found they were not in equal numbers, had no wish to wait for them, nor to fight, for they were near to Vendôme: they made, therefore, for that place, the English pursuing them. Sir Robert de Hangest, cousin to the lord of that name, was slain, and Jean de Mondecris, with five or six others, were made prisoners. The lord de Hangest came so opportunely to the barrier that he found it open. Having fixed his lance, he put himself in a gallant posture of defense: the rest of his companions did so as they came up: however, twelve remained prisoners.

Sir Robert Knolles had also this day made an excursion from the army: he met the lord de Mauvoisin, who defended himself valiantly, but was in the end taken prisoner by Sir Robert himself. This day the army marched by Vendôme to Aussie, and on the morrow to St. Calais, where they halted for two days, and then came to Pontvalin. The English thus advanced, without meeting any to oppose them: but the whole country was full of men-at-arms, and numbers of them were in the city of Mans. At this period, the duke of Anjou passed through Tours, Blois, and Orleans, in his way to Paris; for he had heard his brother was in so dangerous a state that there was no s hope of his recovery, and he was anxious to be with him at his decease. Notwithstanding this illness of the king, from which he was never expected to recover, the men-at-arms did not desist from pursuing and watching the English on their march: the commanders ordered their men to harass them as much they could, and to attempt, if possible, to surround them, which would prevent them from having any provision; and then they would engage with them at their will, whether the king of France gave permission or not. In consequence, the lords of France had brought to that part of the Sarthe that the English were to pass, large beams which they had fixed across the river with sharp stakes, so that they would not be able to cross it. On the banks, they dug very wide and deep ditches, to prevent their descending to the river, or ascending from it.

The earl of Buckingham marched from Pontvalin with his army to the Sarthe, where he halted; for they could not find a ford, as the river was swelled and deep, and difficult to cross except in certain places. The vanguard marched up and down, but could not discover any other ford but where the beams of timber and stakes had been fixed. The lords dismounted, and, observing the ford, said, "It is here we must pass, if we mean to march further: come, let us get to it, and drag these beams out of our way." You would have seen, after this speech, knights, barons, and squires enter the river, and labor most heartily before they could succeed: at last, they gained their point, but with much difficulty, and, having cleared away all obstacles, opened a passage. Had the French been watchful enough, they might have done them much harm; for those who crossed first could not assist those that followed, on account of the deep marshes they had to go through. The English took such pains, that they did pass them, and arrived at Noyon-sur-Sarthe.

CHAPTER LVII.—The death of Charles V, King of France

Johnes 1; 617-8; KL 9: 290

That same day on which the English crossed the Sarthe with so much difficulty, Charles, king of France, departed this life, in his hôtel at Paris called the hôtel de St. Pol. No sooner did his brother, the duke of Anjou, know that the king's eyes were closed than he seized all the jewels of the king, which were very valuable, and had them secured in a safe place, flattering himself they would be of the utmost use to him in the intended war and journey he was about to make; for he already signed himself king of Sicily, Apulia, Calabria and Jerusalem.

The king of France was carried through the city of Paris to the abbey of St. Denis, with his face uncovered, followed by his brothers and his two sons, where he was most honorably interred. He had given orders respecting his burial during his lifetime; and his constable, Sir Bertrand du Guesclin, lies at his feet.

Notwithstanding the orders King Charles had given, before his death, respecting the government of the kingdom, they were totally disregarded; for the duke of Anjou immediately took possession, and overruled all the others. He was willing his nephew should be crowned king, but resolved to have the management of affairs as much, if not more, than any other, on account of his being the eldest uncle; and there were none in the kingdom who dared to dispute it with him. The king of France died on the eve of Michaelmas [September 28]: soon after his decease, the peers and barons of France recommended that the king should be crowned immediately after All Saints [November 1], at Rheims. The three uncles, Anjou, Berry and Burgundy, agreed to this proposal; but they insisted on governing the realm until the child should be of age, that is to say, twenty-one years, which they made the great barons and prelates of France swear to observe. After this, the coronation of the young king was notified in foreign countries, to the duke of Brabant, duke Albert of Bavaria, the count de Savoy, the count de Blois, the duke de Gueldres, the duke de Juliers, the count d'Armagnac, and to the count de Foix. The duke of Bar, the duke of Lorraine, the lord de Couci, the count dauphin of Auvergne, were pursuing the English: they were not, therefore, so soon sent to; but the count of Flanders was invited; and the day fixed was All Saints, which fell on a Sunday.

The men of Ghent were much grieved at the death of the king of France; for he had been very friendly to them during their war, loving but little the earl of Flanders.

We will now speak of the English, and then return to the coronation of the king of France.

The French military disasters at both Crecy (1346) and Poitiers (1356) had plunged the kingdom into political chaos; with nearly half of its lands controlled by Edward the Black Prince, and its king, Jean II, an English captive.

Source: "Battle of Poitiers", From *Grandes Chroniques de France* (c.1415), British Library, Cotton MS Nero E II, f. 166.

When Charles V, called the Wise (1338 - 1380) came to the throne of France in 1364, he inherited a kingdom that had been greatly reduced in land, wealth and prestige, and an aristocracy anxious to prove their mettle on the field of war. Instead, Charles embarked on a policy of avoidance, skirmish and retreat, pledging that he would let the English army "destroy itself." While the policy was both sound and successful, it ran contrary to the notions of chivalry by which France's warrior elite judged themselves, and were judged by both their English counterparts and the peasants they were pledged to protect.

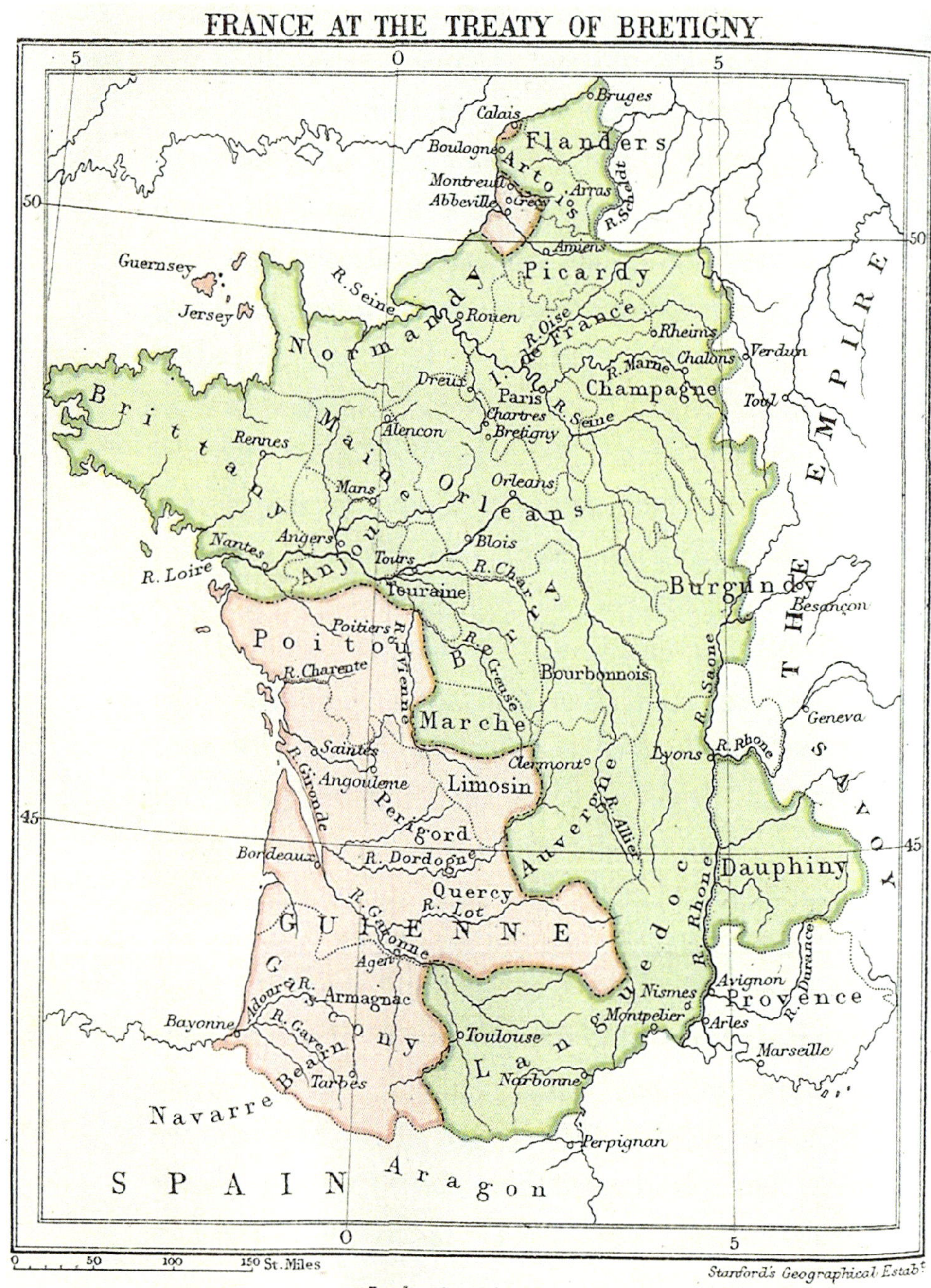

The Treaty of Brétigny was signed on 25 May 1360, between King Edward III of England and King John II (the Good) of France, and can be seen as having marked the end of the first phase of the Hundred Years' War (1337–1453)—as well as the height of English hegemony on the Continent.

Source: From *History of the English People*, Volume 2 (1877); Wikimedia Commons.

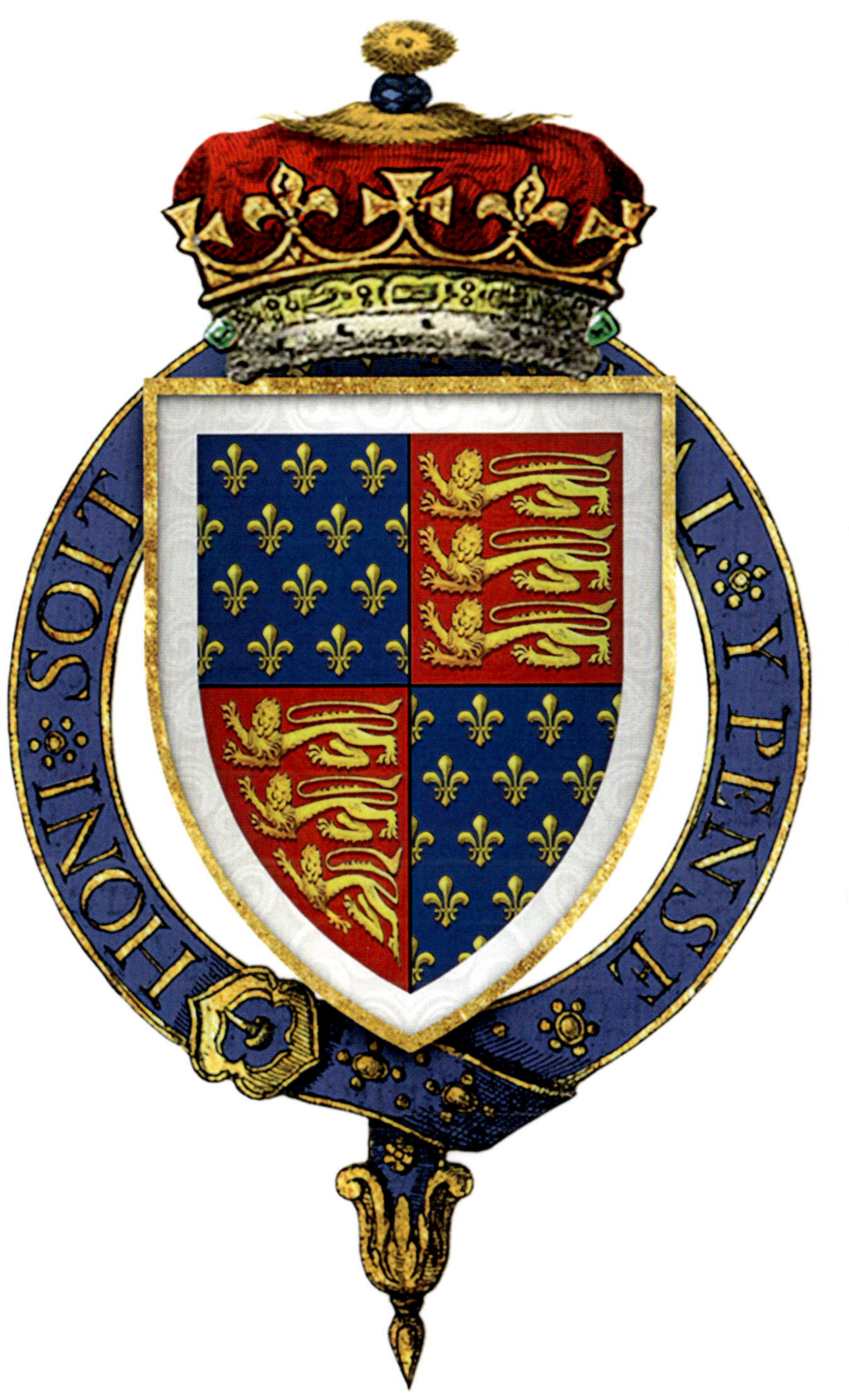

Arms of Thomas of Woodstock, 1st Duke of Gloucester, 1st Earl of Buckingham, 1st Earl of Essex, Duke of Aumale, KG, the fourteenth and youngest child of King Edward III of England and Philippa of Hainault. Buckingham was the leader of the large campaign which followed the Breton War of Succession.

Detail of a miniature of the English landing in Normandy. Although the English-supported claimant, John, duke of Brittany had been victorious, the French had continued to undermine his position and he was later forced into exile in England. An English army was sent under Woodstock to support his position and was ferried to the English continental stronghold of Calais in July 1380. Buckingham's army of 5,200 men were confronted at Troyes by the Duke of Burgundy's army, but under Charles V's new strategy, the French would not offer a pitched battle to the English, so the two armies eventually marched away.

Source: "English troops land in Normandy." From, *Chroniques de France ou de St Denis*, Royal 20 C VII f. 25v

Detail of a miniature of the English landing in Normandy. Although the English-supported claimant, John, duke of Brittany had been victorious in reclaiming the duchy in 1379, the French had continued to undermine his position and he was later forced into exile in England. An English army was sent under Woodstock to support his position and was ferried to the English continental stronghold of Calais in July 1380. Buckingham's army of 5,200 men were confronted at Troyes by the Duke of Burgundy's army, but under Charles V's new strategy, the French would not offer a pitched battle to the English, so the two armies eventually marched away.

Source: "English troops land in Normandy." From, *Chroniques de France ou de St Denis*, Royal 20 C VII f. 25v.

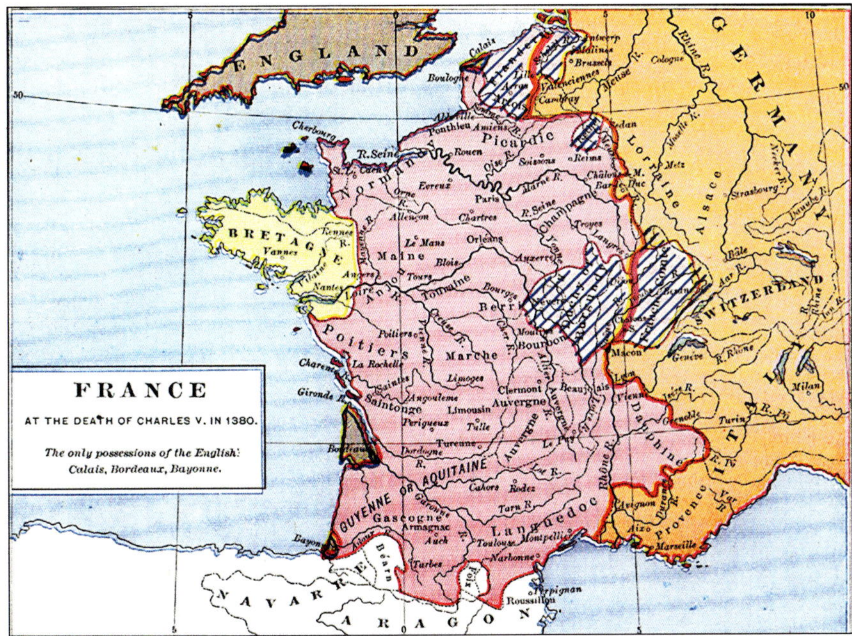

France at the death of Charles V, September 1380. Although his policies had been unpopular, and he did not live to see the collapse of Buckingham's campaign, which he had rightly predicted would "destroy itself", Charles' strategy of avoidance and delay had borne fruit. Coming to the throne with nearly all of southern France in English hands, he left his son, the young Charles VI in control of all but Bordeaux, Bayonne and the northern port of Calais.

In the winter of 1381, the earl of Buckingham realized that his campaign was a failure and broke the siege. But people on both sides still wanted to fight in order to demonstrate their prowess and determination, and Buckingham and his counterpart the constable of France competed over the issuing of safe conducts so that deeds of arms could take place.

In the combats at Vannes, the earl presided over a carefully defined deed where five Englishmen and English partisans would fight five Frenchmen with lances, swords, axes and daggers, all on foot. The day ended in a humiliating defeat for the English.

Source: The Earl of Buckingham (Thomas of Woodstock) and the Duke of Bretagne (John V)preside over foot combat at Vannes; from British Library, Royal Ms. 18 E I f. 139.

Buckingham's failed expedition had been a major effort on the part of the English government to extend and solidify its control over French territory: so major that the taxation associated with it helped cause the English Peasants' Revolt of 1381, a bloody uprising that swept across England.

Source: "Richard II meets with the leaders of the Peasant's Revolt." From a 15th-century copy of Jean Froissart, *Chroniques*, Bibliothèque Nationale de France, 154v.

Buckingham in Brittany (Froissart)

CHAPTER LVIII.—The English arrive in Brittany.—The duke excuses himself for having so long delayed coming to meet them.—They undertake together the siege of Nantes.

Johnes 1: 618-22; KL 9: 292

The English, having crossed the Sarthe in great danger, were not ignorant of the death of the king of France. They were quartered at Noyon sur Sarthe: from thence they marched to Poilli, two leagues from Sablé. The whole strength of France was at that time in the city of Mans, and in that part of the country, but they contented themselves with following the march of the English: some, however, said, they would combat them.

When intelligence of the king's death became public, the intentions of the French were frustrated; for many of the barons decamped, and returned to Paris, to learn what was going forward. The English continued for three days in their quarters: on the fourth day they departed, and came to St. Pierre d'Arne, and from thence to Argentie. The next day the army crossed the river Mayenne, and passed a marsh with much difficulty, for only two or three could march in front for the whole length of this road, which lasted upwards of two leagues. Now, consider what danger they were in; for if the French had known this, and attacked the van, the rear could not have assisted them. The English were greatly afraid of this; however, they passed in safety, and arrived at Cossé, where they halted four days in constant expectation of having some intelligence from Brittany.

The duke of Brittany resided at Hennebon, in the district of Vannes. He had heard frequently of the English, and that they were near the frontiers of Brittany, but he did not know how to act. When he learnt the king of France's death, he took little notice of it, for he did not love him, but said to those near him, "The rancor and hatred which I bore the kingdom of France, on account of this King Charles, is now one-half diminished; for those who hated the father may love the son, and those who have made war on the father may assist the son. It is necessary, however, for me to acquit myself to the English; for, in truth, it has been at my request and solicitation they have marched through the kingdom of France, and I must keep the promises I have made them: but in this there is much difficulty, both in regard to them and me, as I wish our principal towns to shut their gates, and not allow them to enter within them."

The duke then summoned some of his council, such as the lord de Montboursier, Sir Stephen Guyon, Sir William Tanneguy, Sir Eustace de la Houssaye, Sir Geoffry de Kerimel and the judge-assessor of Leon, and said to them: "You will ride to my lord of Buckingham, who is approaching Brittany, and whom I believe you will find not far off: recommend me to him, and salute on my part all his barons. You will tell them, that I shall shortly be at Rennes to meet them; to which place I wish they would direct their march; when we will consider together on the best plans for our further proceedings. Tell them also, that I do not find my country in the same disposition as when I sent to England, which vexes me very much: that, in particular, I am hurt with the men of Nantes, who are more rebellious than any of the others." The knights replied that they would cheerfully carry this message. They took leave of the duke, and rode to Nantes. In the whole, they were about sixty spears.

The English having marched from Cossé, and entered the forest of la Gravelle, which they traversed, arrived at Vitter in Brittany, where they felt themselves more secure than they had hitherto been, for they knew they should no longer be pursued by the French. From thence they went to Chateaubriand, where they remained with the knights from the duke of Brittany, who met them at that place. The earl of Buckingham and the barons of England received the knights from the duke of Brittany most honorably, and there were many councils and debates. The English said in plain terms, that they were astonished that neither the duke nor the country were better prepared, and showed no inclination to receive them; for it was at their request that they had come, and had suffered so many difficulties in their march through France.

The lord de Montboursier then said, in excuse of the duke, "My lords, you have very good cause for having thus spoken, and the duke has a thorough good will to fulfill every article of the engagements which have been entered into between you both, to the utmost of his power; but he cannot act as he wishes. In particular, the inhabitants of Nantes, which is the key to Brittany, are in complete rebellion, and are ready to receive men-at-arms from France. This conduct has very much astonished my lord; for it was that town which first entered into the alliance with the other chief towns in Brittany, and my lord believes that the men of Nantes have entered into a new treaty with the young king of France, who is to be crowned on All Saints Day ensuing. My lord, therefore, begs and entreats you will hold him excused: he also desires that you will take the road to Rennes, where he will come to meet you; for he has a great desire to see you, and will not fail to be there." These words much pleased the earl of Buckingham and the English: they declared, he could not say more. The messengers, returning to the duke towards Hennebon, met him at Vannes. The English continued four days at Chateaubriand, when they marched away to the suburbs of Rennes: the gates of the city were shut, and no man-at-arms was allowed to enter: the earl of Buckingham, however, was lodged in the town, as were the lord Latimer, Sir Robert Knolles, and five or six other barons of the council to the earl. They remained there upwards of fifteen days, waiting in vain for the duke, who never came, which greatly astonished them.

The lord de Monteraulieu, the lord Montfort of Brittany, Sir Geoffry de Kerimel, and Sir Alain de la Houssaye, the governor of Rennes, were in the city, as also Sir Eustace, the governor's brother, who made daily excuses for the duke. I don't know whether they had a good cause to plead, but the English began to be very discontented with the duke for not coming. The people of Nantes kept their gates well-guarded; for they did not think themselves secure from the English, whom they knew to be at Rennes: they sent, therefore, to the duke of Anjou, who had been the origin of the late treaties, and by whom the greater part of the kingdom was governed, to remonstrate with him on their incapacity to defend themselves, if they should be besieged, without having a stronger body of men-at-arms: they therefore entreated him to provide them with reinforcements. The four dukes who governed France, Anjou, Berry, Burgundy and Bourbon, complied with their request, and sent upwards of six hundred good and valorous men-at-arms. Thus was Nantes reinforced. Those men-at-arms immediately repaired every part of the walls, and put the town in a proper condition to resist a siege or an attack, if such should happen.

The English, quartered at Rennes and thereabouts, began to despair because the duke did not come to them: they resolved, in a council, to send to find out his reasons for delay. Lord Thomas Percy and Sir Thomas Trivet were ordered to wait on him, escorted by five hundred lances, to prevent or oppose any ambuscades which might be laid for them. These two barons departed from Rennes, attended by this body of lances, with as many archers, and took the road to Hennebon. They set out on a Thursday: the following Saturday, the earl marched the army to St. Sulpice in Brittany, where he halted three days: on the fourth, he marched to Combront, where he remained four days. The duke of Brittany had left Hennebon, and was at Vannes. He had regular information of all the English were doing, and, after having well considered everything, resolved to go to them: for his own honor, and the alliances he had formed with them, would not allow him to delay longer. Having learned that Sir Robert Knolles, lord Thomas Percy and Sir Thomas Trivet were coming to him, he began his journey to Rennes; and, the day that he set out from Vannes, he met the English knights. This meeting caused great joy: the duke of Brittany made inquiries after the earl of Buckingham, and the knights told him they had left him very melancholy at Rennes, because he had not any tidings of him. The duke excused himself by saying, that by his faith he could not help it. They then rode all together to Vannes, where they were well received; but they knew that the English army had marched from Combront to la Hedé and la Maisiere, for they had followed that road.

The earl of Buckingham arrived at Vannes the next day, when great affection was shown on both sides. The duke handsomely excused himself to the earl and the English for his delay in coming to them: he said that he did not find his country determined to perform what they had promised him at the beginning of the summer.

The earl replied: "Fair brother of Brittany, it shall not be long, if you follow my advice, before you punish these rebels; for, with the forces which you have yourself, and those we have brought, with the additional reinforcements that may arrive from England every day, we shall bring your subjects into such a state of submission that they will gladly throw themselves on your mercy." With these and suchlike speeches they conversed for a long time, when each retired to his hôtel. On the morrow, they rode out together: it was then settled that the council of the earl should attend the duke to Rennes, and finally make arrangements for their future proceedings. That evening the duke, with the earl's council, remained at la Maisiere, and the earl returned to la Hedé, for they were all quartered in the environs of la Maisiere. The next day, the duke went to Rennes, accompanied by the lord Latimer, Sir Robert Knolles, lord Thomas Percy, Sir Thomas Trivet, and others of the council of the earl.

They remained three days in consultation at Rennes: at last, it was determined, and sworn to, on the part of the duke of Brittany, on the holy Evangelists, that he would lay siege to Nantes, in company with the earl of Buckingham, and be there in person fifteen days after the English were arrived. The duke also engaged to send down the river Loire plenty of barges, the more to constrain those of Nantes, and would not himself quit the place, nor allow his army to do so, before it should be conquered. The earl of Buckingham was sent to la Hedé, that all this business might be completely settled; and that he might be present at these councils. The army therefore decamped, and took up their former quarters in the suburbs of Rennes. The earls and barons entered Rennes, where the earl gave them a most magnificent dinner. The duke of Brittany engaged and swore by his faith solemnly on the holy Evangelists to come to Nantes with all his forces. After this, he returned to Hennebon. The English remained for upwards of fifteen days at Rennes, making the necessary preparations.

The inhabitants of Nantes, being informed that the siege of their town was intended, took every precaution to defend themselves. One of the principal captains in Nantes was Sir Jean le Barrois des Barres, a valiant and expert knight: there were with him the following captains; Jean de Clisson, Jean de Châteaumorand, Morfonace, Sir Jean de Malatrait, the lord de Tournemine and several more, all the flower of the army. These leaders made very prudent and able defenses, as well towards the river as at the gates, walls and towers which were opposite to the plain, and at those parts where they thought it probable an attack might be made.

We will now give these affairs a respite, and speak of the ceremonies of the coronation of the young King Charles, who at this period was crowned at Rheims.

CHAPTER LIX.—The Coronation of King Charles VI of France

Johnes 1; 620-2; KL 9: 300

As you may well imagine, nothing was spared by the nobility and great lords to add to the magnificence of the coronation of the young King Charles of France, who was crowned at Rheims on a Sunday, in the twelfth year of his age, in the year 1380. At this solemnity there were many high and mighty lords: his uncles of Anjou, Berry, Burgundy and Bourbon, were present; as were also his great uncles, Wenceslaus duke of Brabant, the duke of Bar, the duke of Lorraine, the count de Savoy, the count de la Marche, the count d'Eu and Sir William de Namur: but the earl of Flanders and the count de Blois sent excuses. There were several other lords whom I cannot name.

The young king made his entry into the city of Rheims on the Saturday, handsomely attended by the great lords, nobility and minstrels, at Vespers. In particular, there were upwards of thirty trumpets, which preceded him, and sounded so clear it was quite marvelous to hear them. The young king of France dismounted before the church of Our Lady at Rheims, in company with his uncles and brother. There were also his cousins of Navarre, d'Albret, of Bar and of Harcourt, and a great many other young squires, children of the great barons of France, whom the king on the morrow, being the day of his coronation, created knights. This Saturday, the king heard Vespers in the church of Our Lady, and performed his vigils in that church, according to the custom of those times, the greater part of the night. All the youths desirous of knighthood attended him, and did the same.

On the Sunday, which was All Saints Day, the church of Our Lady was very richly decorated for the coronation; so much so that it could not possibly have been better ordered.

The archbishop of Rheims, after having said mass with great solemnity, consecrated the king with the holy ampulla with which St. Remy had anointed Clovis, the first Christian king of the French. This sacred oil was sent from God by a holy angel, with which the kings of France have ever since been anointed, and it never diminishes. Now this must be considered as wonderfully miraculous.

Before the consecration, the king created, in front of the altar, all those young squires, knights. The office of mass was afterwards chanted by the archbishop, the king being clothed in his royal robes, and seated on an elevated throne, adorned with cloth of gold; and all the young knights were placed on low benches, covered also with the same, at his feet. In this state they remained the whole day. The new constable, Sir Olivier de Clisson, was present; he had been named constable a few days prior to this ceremony, and performed well his charge and everything belonging to it. The principal barons of France were also there so richly dressed it would be tedious to relate: the king was seated in royal majesty, with a crown on his head rich and precious beyond measure. The church of Our Lady at Rheims was so crowded during this ceremony that one could not turn one's foot. I have heard also, that at this accession of the young king to the throne, in order to please the people of France, all impositions, aids, taxes, subsidies and other levies, which had displeased and had much oppressed them, were abolished, greatly to the joy of the subjects.

After mass, they went to the palace; but, as the hall was too small for such numbers, they erected in the court of the palace a large covered stage, on which the dinner was served. The king was seated with his five uncles of Brabant, Anjou, Berry, Burgundy and Bourbon; but, though they were at his table, they were at a distance from him. The archbishop of Rheims and other prelates were on his right hand. He was served by the great barons, the lord de Couci, the lord de Clisson, Sir Guy de la Trémouille, the lord high admiral and several others, on handsome horses, covered and decorated with gold brocade. The whole day passed in ceremonies. On the morrow, many of the great barons took leave of the king and his uncles, and returned to their own country. The king went that day to dinner at the abbey of St. Thierry, two leagues from Rheims; for those monks are bound to give him this entertainment, and the city of Rheims to provide for the coronation of the king. Thus ended this noble feast. He returned to Paris, where he was grandly feasted by the Parisians at his entrance.

After all these ceremonies, entertainments and honors, there were great councils held on the present and future administration of the kingdom. It was settled that the duke of Berry should have the government of Languedoc; the duke of Burgundy, Picardy and Normandy; and that the duke of Anjou should remain near the king's person, and have, in fact, the whole government of the realm. The count de St. Pol was recalled, who had been banished from the favor of the late King Charles. He was indebted for this grace to Wenceslaus duke of Brabant, and to the duke of Anjou, in whose affection the count de St. Pol was. He immediately left Han sur Heure, situated in the bishopric of Liege, where he had remained a long time, and returned to France, leaving his lady in the castle of Bouhaing. All the confiscations were taken off his estates, which reverted to his profit.

We will say no more on these subjects, but return to the affairs of Brittany and the earl of Buckingham.

CHAPTER LX.—The earl of Buckingham besieges Nantes.—Sallies are made by the garrison.

Johnes 1: 624-5; KL 9: 303

You have heard of the agreement that had been sworn to, between the duke of Brittany and earl of Buckingham, to besiege Nantes. When the duke had left Rennes, the lord de Montboursier, Sir Stephen Guyon, the lord de la Houssaye and their company retired to Vannes and Hennebon; and the earl of Buckingham and his army prepared to march to Nantes: they set out, therefore, from the suburbs of Rennes, and the adjacent villages where they had been quartered, and lodged that day at Chastillon, on the next day at Bain, and the third at Nozay: and on the fourth they quartered themselves in the suburbs of Nantes. The earl was lodged at the gate of Sauvetout: the lord Latimer constable of the army, lord Fitzwalter and lord Basset were quartered at the gate of St. Nicholas, close to the riverside. Sir William Windsor and Sir Hugh Calverley were lodged right honorably among their own men, as was proper for them.

In the town were numbers of knights and squires from Brittany, Beauce, Anjou and Maine, who well understood how to defend the place: they had the whole load and charge, for the inhabitants gave themselves no trouble about it. It happened, that on Martinmas eve [November 10], Sir Jean le Barrois des Barres collected some of his companions in the town and said to them; "My good gentlemen, we know that our enemies are close to us, and we have not yet given them an alert: I am of opinion, that this fine night we should look at them, and give them a skirmish." "By my faith," they replied, "you speak loyally: tell us what you wish, and we will do it."

They collected a body of about one hundred and twenty well-armed and determined men. They ordered the gate to be opened where the constable, the lord Basset and the lord Fitzwalter were quartered, and placed foot guards at it to secure their retreat. The leaders of this troop were Barrois des Barres, Jean Châteaumorand and the captain de Clisson. They came so unexpectedly that they found the English at supper: having shouted their war-cry, "Des Barres!" the French began to lay about them, slaying and wounding many. The English were soon prepared and drawn up before their quarters. When the French saw this they very prudently retreated in a compact body towards the town. The English came from all parts to the skirmish: some of each side were struck to the ground, and the French driven within their barriers. There were some slain and wounded on both sides; but Barrois des Barres entered the town with so little loss that this skirmish was held, both at home and abroad, as a gallant action.

On the evening of St. Martin's Day [November 11], Barrois des Barres spoke to his companions, saying, "It would be a good thing if, at day-break tomorrow, we could get six or seven large barges, with two hundred men and the same number of crossbows, to visit our enemies by water; for they have not the least suspicions of our coming to them down the river." They all assented to this proposal, and assembled that same night the number of men des Barres had fixed on: before daylight, they embarked in six large boats, and, floating down the stream, landed below the enemy's quarters. Sir John Harlestone and his men were lodged in a large hôtel, not far from where they had landed, and at day-break they surrounded and attacked it. Sir John was soon dressed and armed, as were his men: they defended themselves courageously, the archers shooting at the crossbows. This skirmish was long and severe: many were killed and wounded, and Sir John would have been conquered, if Sir Robert Knolles, who was quartered not far distant, had not armed himself and his men, and, with displayed banner, advanced hastily to his assistance. Sir William Windsor did the same, who, having had information of what was going on, hurried thither;

besides, the English were now coming from all directions. The French retreated to their boats, as they saw the necessity of it, or else of risking the event of a battle. There was much skirmishing on the shore, as they re-embarked, but they departed very gallantly. The captains performed many valorous deeds; but, on their return to Nantes, several of the French were taken, slain or drowned. All who heard of this enterprise considered it as one of great courage and ability.

The English, finding themselves thus constantly attacked by the garrison of Nantes, resolved to be more on their guard, and to keep a stricter watch. The seventh night, however, after the attack that Barrois had led down the river, he made another sally from the gate where the earl of Buckingham was quartered; Barrois had with him about two hundred men-at-arms and one hundred cross-bows. The Germans were on guard this night, under the command of Sir Algars and Sir Thomas de Roddes. Barrois, Jean de Châteaumorand and de Clisson, with their men, immediately attacked this guard of Germans, when a sharp fight began, and many were struck to the earth. Those quartered near to the earl arose, armed themselves, and hastened to this skirmish; but, when Barrois saw the numbers increasing, he retreated to the gate, fighting all the way. Several were killed by the arrows, and many wounded on both sides. Sir Thomas de Roddes, a knight from Germany, was struck by an arrow, which pierced quite through his helmet to his head; of which wound he died three days after: it was a pity, for he was a very able knight. The French and Bretons re-entered Nantes with scarcely any loss, carrying with them six prisoners.

Things remained in this state, and the English much on their guard, for they expected an alert every night.

CHAPTER LXI.—The duke of Brittany explains his reasons for not coming to the siege of Nantes.—The garrison continue most valiantly to make sallies.

Johnes 1: 625-7; KL 9: 308

The earl of Buckingham remained in this situation before Nantes, daily expecting the arrival of the duke of Brittany, who never came, nor kept any of the promises he had engaged to perform, which quite discouraged the English, who did not know what to think of it. They sent repeatedly messengers with letters, to remonstrate with him badly he was conducting himself by not keeping those promises and agreements he had sworn to so solemnly when in the city of Rennes. To all these letters the earl did not receive one answer: the English had to think that the messengers had been slain, for none returned; and in truth there was great danger to all who travelled between Nantes and Hennebon, unless they were strongly escorted. The roads were so strictly guarded by men-at-arms, no one could pass without being taken, or his business known; and, if there were found upon him letters from the English to the duke, or from the duke to them, the bearer was sure to be put to death. In addition to this, the foragers of the army dared not venture abroad but in large companies; for the knights and squires of the country had assembled, and would not suffer their lands to be overrun and pillaged, so that, whenever they fell in with bodies of twenty or thirty, they took all they had and their horses from them, besides wounding or killing them. This enraged the army, but they did not know on whom to revenge themselves.

To tell the truth, the duke of Brittany did everything he could to make his people consent to follow him to the siege of Nantes, according to the agreement he had entered into with the earl of Buckingham at Rennes: but he could not succeed. Even the barons, knights, and squires told him plainly they would not assist in the destruction of their country for the sake of England, and would never arm themselves in his behalf so long as the English remained in Brittany. The duke upon this remonstrated with them, and asked why they had desired him to send for the aid of the English. They told him that it was more to give alarm to the king of France and his council, that they might not be deprived of their ancient privileges, than for anything else; and, in case the king of France wished them no ill will, they would not make war against him. The duke could not obtain any other answer.

On the other hand, the lord de Clisson, constable of France, the lord de Dînant, the lord de Laval, the viscount de Rohan, the lord de Rochefort, and all the great barons of Brittany, had their castles well-fortified and guarded. They told the duke, or sent word to him by messengers, that he had best consider well what he was about; for he had been ill advised in sending for the English, and bringing them over to destroy and carry war into his country: that he must not expect any aid from them: therefore, if he should go to Nantes, to assist in the siege, as they had heard it to be his intention, and which he ought not to have promised, they would attack his country on all sides, and would give him so much employment that he should not know what he ought to attend to first: but, if he were willing to acknowledge the king of France, and place himself under his obedience, as he was bound to do, they engaged to make his peace with the young king. They added that those who had had the courage to oppose the deceased King Charles might be beloved by the king his son. Such was the treatment the duke met with from the great lords of Brittany, so that, in fact, he did not know what to do; for he found he could not place any security on his barons or subjects: it therefore behooved him to dissemble.

The siege of Nantes still continued; and on the day of Our Lady in Advent, the French garrison resolved to make another attack on the besiegers, for they had left them quiet for some time. Sir Amaury de Clisson, cousin-german to the lord de Clisson, and the lord d'Amboise, made an assault, with about two hundred spears, on the quarters of Sir William Windsor. They sallied out at the gate of Richebourg, on the river side, where Sir Hugh Calverley's men were that night on guard. The lord d'Amboise was made a knight by Sir Amaury de Clisson. These men-at-arms, French and Bretons, advanced in high spirits to the ford, and gained it, though they found it guarded by Sir William Cossington, and a sharp contest ensued, in which many a man was overthrown. Sir William Windsor and Sir Hugh Calverley were in their quarters, and, hearing the noise, armed themselves and issued forth to the midst of the tumult, where the conflict mightily increased: both parties behaved valiantly. The French and Bretons made good their retreat, fighting all the way, and re-entered the gate of Richebourg with little loss: they had taken prisoner a knight with ten men-at-arms, and had had only three of their men taken.

On Thursday before Christmas Eve, Barrois des Barres, with the lord de Solete and six score men-at-arms, made another sally from the gate of Sauvetout, to beat up the quarters of the earl of Buckingham: the earl of Devonshire had that night the command of the guard. The engagement was very severe, and many were thrown down and wounded by spears; but the English, being in greater force than their enemies, drove them back to their barriers: they lost, in killed and prisoners, sixteen. In this attack, an English knight, called Sir Hugh Kitiel, received a blow on his helmet, with a bolt, that caused his death.

Every man then retired to his quarters, and nothing more was done that night; but the captains in Nantes held a council, and resolved on Christmas Eve to make a sally with the whole garrison. The earl of Buckingham and the other English were kept in constant alarm by the garrison, and the foragers had many difficulties in providing provender for the horses, for they dared not forage but in large companies. The earl and his council were much astonished that the duke of Brittany did not come or send them any intelligence, so that they began to be very discontented. Upon considering everything, they concluded that he had given them very weak support on all occasions, which they could not account for, nor did they know how to seek redress for it. They therefore determined to send once more Sir Robert Knolles, lord Thomas Percy, and Sir Thomas Trivet, to Vannes or Hennebon, to remonstrate with him on the part of the earl, how very ill he had conducted himself in not having fulfilled his engagements with greater honor. This resolution was afterwards broken; for, when they more maturely weighed it, they found they could not send off this detachment without weakening their army too much, and that they could not go to the duke but with the whole army; for, if they should march only five or six hundred lances, and meet with a thousand or fifteen hundred, the odds would be too great, and they would be slain: they therefore did not detach any part of their army.

When Christmas Eve arrived Barrois des Barres, Sir Amaury de Clisson, the lord d'Amboise, the lord de Solete, the châtelain de Clisson, Jean de Châteaumorand, and all the captains in Nantes sallied forth in the evening through St. Peter's gate, with a determination to act well, accompanied by six hundred men-at-arms. On passing the gate, they formed themselves into two divisions; one of which marched down the street, and the other through the fields, towards the quarters of the lord Latimer and the lord Fitzwalter. Sir Evan Fitzwarren and Sir William Renton commanded the [English] guard. On the first attack, they [the French] gained the barriers of the guard, and, killing many, they drove them as far as the quarters of the constable, lord Latimer. They halted before the hôtel of the lord Delawarr, where there was a grand engagement; for the French had the intention of conquering this hôtel, which they were on the point of taking and the lord Delawarr in it. The guard suffered much before any reinforcements arrived. Sir Evan Fitzwarren, the lord Delawarr, and Sir William Drayton, did many gallant deeds. These assaults caused the battalions of the constable and marshal to exert themselves: they sounded their trumpets, and armed immediately. Sir William Windsor and Sir Hugh Calverley, hearing the trumpets, knew the vanguard was engaged: they ordered their trumpets to sound also, and a number of torches to be lighted and their banners displayed, with which they marched to the place where the combat was, attended by one hundred men-at-arms and as many archers. In another part, Sir Thomas Trivet, lord Thomas Percy, and lord Basset, each with their banners before them, advanced to the skirmish. The vanguard needed all the haste they could make to relieve the guard, for they were on the point of losing their quarters: but when these barons and their men were arrived, they drove back the French and Bretons, who, forming together in a handsome body, retreated towards the town, skirmishing all the way. Many valiant deeds were done; and some young French knights and squires, in order to gain honors, ventured too far, so that Sir Tristan de la Jaille was taken, in his foolish attempt, by a squire from Hainault called Thierry de Sommain.

Thus was this attack made. All those, or at least a part, who had come from Nantes, re-entered it; for, in these cases, there must be wounded and slain; and, when the heat of an engagement animates, such accidents are to be expected. They returned, however, without much loss; for they had full as many prisoners from the English as they had had taken from them. When the gates were closed, they attended to their wounded. The army returned to their quarters, but did not dismiss the guard: on the contrary, additions were made to it.

No sally was attempted on Christmas Day, nor on the succeeding feasts. The English expected to be attacked every night; but what troubled them the most was their not receiving any intelligence from the duke of Brittany. Their provisions were become very short, for it was with difficulty they could forage. The garrison was well supplied, by means of the river Loire, from the rich countries of Poitou, Saintonge, and La Rochelle.

CHAPTER LXII.—The English break up the siege of Nantes.—The duke of Brittany sends handsome excuses to the earl of Buckingham.

Johnes 1: 627-30; KL 9: 314

After the earl of Buckingham and the English had been before Nantes two months and four days, they found they could gain nothing, and that the duke of Brittany would not keep any of his engagements, for he neither came nor sent word to them. They thought it best to decamp (since they could not succeed), and march towards Vannes, to have some conversation with the duke, and know from himself the reasons of his conduct. Orders were issued for the army to pack up and depart: they decamped, the last day of the year, in the same order of battle with which they had marched through France, and halted, the day they left Nantes, at Nort, where they remained for three days, on account of the bridge being broken down. They had much trouble in repairing this bridge, so that their carriages might pass over: however, it was made good and strong, and the army, having also crossed the river Vilaine on a Saturday, took up their quarters at Lohéac, where they stayed two days. When the army left Lohéac, they quartered themselves at Gosselin, where they also halted for two days, and then they came to la Trinité. They crossed the river Aust at the Pont de Boquinio, when the whole army stopped on that side of the water on the plains.

The inhabitants of Vannes received exact information of the day on which the army decamped, and when they crossed the river, from the country people, and that the earl of Buckingham was marching his army towards them, intending to fix his quarters in their city. They did not know what to do, whether to permit them to come into their town or not. They therefore went to the duke at Hennebon; but the day they set out they met him, two leagues from Vannes, on his road thither. The duke perceiving his good subjects advancing towards him, asked them what was the news, and where they were going. "My lord," they replied, "as for news, we can tell you enough: the earl of Buckingham and the English are marching this way; and it is their intention, as we have been informed, to quarter themselves in your good town of Vannes. Now, you must consider how you would have us act; for without your order we will not do anything. In truth, they have repaired the Pont de Boquinio, which was broken down."

The duke, on hearing these words, paused a little, and then answered, "God help us! Do not you be uneasy nor alarmed at trifles, for everything will turn out well. These English will not do you any harm. I have entered into certain engagements which I must perform, and acquit myself to them. I am now going to Vannes; and tomorrow, as I verily believe, they will arrive there. I will advance to meet my brother, the earl, and will pay him every honor and respect in my power, for truly I am bound so to do. As for the rest, you will act according to my advice, which is, that you meet him, and present him the keys of your town, saying, that you and all the town are ready to receive him and to obey his orders, on condition that he swear, fifteen days after he shall be requested to depart, he will march out of the town, and will return the keys. This is the best advice I can give you." The citizens of Vannes replied, "My lord, we will obey your directions." They then rode on together to Vannes, where the duke lodged that night; and the English fixed their quarters at St. Jean, a small village, situated two leagues from Vannes.

The earl of Buckingham received that evening letters from the duke, written with great affection, welcoming him to the neighborhood of Vannes. On the morrow, when the earl had heard mass, and drank a cup, he mounted his horse, and with his whole army marched in great order towards Vannes; first the vanguard, then the earl in the center battalion, the rearguard following close upon him. In this order they met the duke of Brittany, who had come out a long league from Vannes to meet them. The duke and earl showed great affection to each other. After this reception, which was very honorable, they rode together, the earl on the right and the duke on the left, and entered into conversation: the earl said, "By holy Mary, fair brother of Brittany, we waited most impatiently for your arrival at Nantes, during the siege, according to the treaty entered into between you and me, and yet you never came." "By my faith, my lord," answered the duke, " I could not any way accomplish it; and I must own to you that I have been exceedingly enraged about that, but it was not possible for me to act otherwise; for my subjects, notwithstanding every argument I could use, in remonstrating with them on the treaties I had made with you at their own requests, would never agree to march to assist you in the siege of Nantes. The principal barons kept themselves ready prepared on the borders, such as the lord de Clisson, the lord de Dînant, the lord d'Orval, the viscount de Rohan, and the lord de Rochefort, to guard the entrances of Brittany. All of those adherents and friends of mine, knights and prelates and principal towns, are this moment in a state of rebellion; at which I am very much mortified, for by their misconduct you have reason to find fault with me. I will tell you, therefore, my lord, what you shall do: being now the depth of winter, it is cold and uncomfortable to keep an army in the field: you shall come to Vannes, where you will remain until April or May, to recover yourselves from your fatigues, and I will give orders that your men are taken care of. You will pass your time as well as you can, and in the summer we will revenge ourselves for all this disrespect."

The earl replied, "May God assist us," for he saw plainly there was nothing better to be expected. The duke conducted him towards Vannes, when the inhabitants of the town came out in their robes, and, addressing the earl, said to him in an amicable manner, "My lord, out of respect to your lordship, and in reverence to your great honor, we have not any objections to your entering our town; but we wish, in order to satisfy the people (otherwise you will not be very secure), you would swear to us, on the holy Evangelists, that fifteen days after we ask you to depart, you will march away with your whole army, without doing or suffering to be done to us the least molestation." "By my faith, none shall be done to you," answered the earl of Buckingham; "and I will swear and keep it." They afterwards made the other lords swear on their faith, and on the holy Evangelists, to keep the same engagement as the earl had done, to which they readily assented. It behooved them so to do, unless they had wished to sleep in the fields. The division of the army of the earl of Buckingham was quartered in the town of Vannes, and himself lodged in the hôtel of the duke, a well built and pleasantly situated castle, called la Motte.

The duke of Brittany entertained the English knights handsomely at dinner in his castle of la Motte, and then retired to Sucinio, where he resided; but sometimes he came to Vannes to visit the earl and hold conferences with him, and then returned to the place whence he had come. lord Latimer, lord Fitzwalter, lord Thomas Percy, Sir Thomas Trivet, and the whole of the van of the army, were to have been quartered at Hennebon; but the inhabitants would not open their gates to them, so that they were forced to lodge themselves in the suburbs and in the fields.

Sir Robert Knolles and lord Fitzwarren, with many more, were to have been quartered in Quimpercorentin; but the inhabitants treated them as those of Hennebon had done, and they were obliged to make the same shifts with the van. Sir William Windsor and the rearward were, by orders of the duke, to lodge at Quimperlé; but they could not, by entreaties or threats, prevail on the inhabitants to open their gates. In consequence, they suffered much from the inclemency of the weather and the ill-usage they met with: what was not worth three farthings was sold to them for twelve, and they could hardly get any provision at such prices. Their horses perished through cold and famine, for they did not know where to collect forage; and, when they went out to seek it, they were in great peril, as the adjacent countries were all inimical to them.

The viscount de Rohan possessed at that time two strong castles in the neighborhood of Vannes; one was called Caire, and the other Linguighant. In these two castles, the viscount had strong garrisons, which, aided by other garrisons of the lord de Clisson situated on this frontier, such as châteaux Josselin, Montagu, and Moncontour, did much mischief to the English foragers, killing many. The duke of Brittany could not prevent this; for the lord de Clisson, constable of France, carried on the war in the name of the king of France, and had in the country numerous bodies of men-at-arms, so that the English dared not stir abroad in small parties. When it is considered that they were encamped in the fields, without any entrenchments, it is marvelous they did not suffer great losses; for those quartered in Vannes could not easily assist those near Quimperlé, Hennebon, or Quimpercorentin. To say the truth, the duke stood boldly forward, and guarded them to the best of his abilities, to prevent their destruction. He fairly told his council, that he had but poorly acquitted himself towards the earl and his army of all the promises he had made them.

At this time, there were four great barons at Paris, whom the duke had sent to the king of France to make his peace; the viscount de Rohan, Sir Charles de Dinan, Sir Guy lord de Laval, and Sir Guy lord de Rochefort. These four barons of Brittany had remonstrated with him in council, during the time the earl of Buckingham was before Nantes, several times, and with much wisdom, in such terms as these: "My lord, you show to all the world, that your heart is entirely given to the English: you have brought into this country Englishmen who, if they gain the upper hand, will diminish your inheritance. What profit or pleasure can you have in this great affection for them? Look to the situation of the king of Navarre, who put his confidence in them: after having given them possession of his town and castle of Cherbourg, they have never quitted it, nor ever will, but keep it as their own property. Therefore, if you put them into any of your fortified towns in Brittany, they will not leave them, for daily reinforcements will arrive. See how they keep Brest; nor have they any thought of surrendering it, although it is your inheritance. Be satisfied, my lord, with the love of the people of this country, who will never give up the king of France to serve and belong to the king of England. If your duchess is from England, would you, for that, run the risk of losing your whole dukedom, which has cost you so much to gain, and always continue in a state of warfare? In case the country should be against you, you will be but as one man. Quit your present advisers; for the king of France whom you did not love is dead, and at present there is a young and amiable monarch on the throne, who has good abilities; and those who have hated the father may serve the son. We undertake to make your peace with him, and bring you to a proper understanding with each other. You will continue lord and duke of Brittany with great power, and the English return to their own country." In such words as the above, and others well glossed over, had these barons remonstrated several times with the duke. They had succeeded so far as to have half gained his consent to their purpose; but he still dissembled with the king of France and the English, as well as with his own council, until he should more plainly see what would be the event.

The earl of Buckingham and his barons were ignorant of all these secret intrigues which the four barons above mentioned were carrying on at Paris with the king and his uncles, until the matter was arranged. Prior to their knowledge of it, and before they left Brittany, there were a deed of arms and a combat held at Vannes, in the presence of the earl of Buckingham and the lords who were there, of which I will speak; for it is not a thing that I ought to be silent about, nor should it be forgotten.

The Siege of Nantes (Cabaret)

XLII. How the people occupying Nantes for the King of France fought against the English.

CBD 124-7

Day and knight, the men-at-arms sent to Nantes for the King of France, and the duke of Bourbon, together with Sir Pierre de Bueilh, did not cease to think how they could harm the English who besieged them. So it happened one day, that among the castle all of the company of the duke of Bourbon and the lord of Bueilh went out and they went to strike the guard of the English, Sir Estienne de Cusanton, who was in lodgings at Saulsaye, around matins, the changing of the guard. And the French charged right into them, and there were a good 150 English men-at-arms, and just as many French, and in this encounter, one party of the English was taken and the other fled and they held captive the captain Sir Estienne de Cusanton, one of the most valiant knights of England, and thirty-six men-at-arms of his; and there were a good sixty killed. And he ran well into the lodgings. And the English put themselves in battle order before, which profited them little, for the companions pushed them inside and freely led away from Nantes their prisoners, and sixty horses of carriage; and some good equipment was gained and this was the first sally they made from Nantes. And before the camp of the Hainaulters who were at the other of the gates, where they had valiant men that is to say the lord of Vertains, the canon of Robessart, Thierry de Semain, the bastard of Vertains, and the young men of Maubeuge who amounted to a good 300 combatants and lodged near the ditches in the strong houses of the bourgeois, and they commenced to dig a mine, because the Hainaulters are by custom good miners, and they mined well for the space of 10 days, so the French counter-mined to intercept it. And these mines were so alike that one was able to converse with the other. As the mines continued, it happened that the day was Christmas Eve and some of those from Nantes had taken a man, a Gascon, who told the French captains how the Hainaulters did not intend to do anything that night except play dice in the house of the Lord of Vertains. So they had the idea to open the gate which was close to them, and attack them inside and so that was done. And on Christmas Eve at the hour of midnight the companions of Nantes, who were a good 700 combatants, struck heartily at the camp of the Hainaulters, who were enjoying themselves at dice and they defeated them and spoiled them and those who were killed included Thierry de Semain, and one of the youths of Maubeuge, and the bastard of Vertains and a good sixty men-at-arms, and they took twenty-six good prisoners. And among those who were killed of the insiders was Mace des Ymaiges, and there Sir Tristan de Jaille and Pierre de Sury of the house of the duke of Bourbon, and Robert Guy were taken prisoner; and the Hainaulters retreated into a high house for safety and their camp was overrun and many of the duke of Bourbon's people were wounded, that all was gained and thus went the day. So the companions retreated inside Nantes: for this time, they didn't go any further and the next day they recovered their prisoners in exchange for others, and their mine was broken, about which they did not do any more on this side. And after four days the marshal of Savoy, Sir Boniface de Chalant, wrote some letters to Châteaumorand and Barrois, who received him in their company, for he had thirty men-at-arms, gentlemen, and because they knew him to be a good knight they sent to fetch him and there was a good company inside the city. And Sir Boniface having come, they resolved to inform the lord of Bueilh, Châteaumorand, Sir Le Barrois and the others who had led, how they had been able to do damage to the camp of the earl of Buckingham, chief and principal captain of that people who were lodged before the gate in Richebourg, and he had made his barrier out of two wagons because when the English saw them open the gate they pulled back just to their barrier and when they did not open it they stayed in their house to shoot. So they advised one day that those inside should make a mine under the gate that the English might not see them lower the bridge and that they and their people would be able to hide in the ditches without being seen by the others. So it was done and one day after dinner they rushed into the ditches of their embankments, 400 men-at-arms and 300 good arbalesters of the garrison of Nantes, in an ambush; and they lowered the bridge and sent out 100 men-at-arms, to make it appear they were going to skirmish at the barrier, as was the custom. And just as the English came up to their barrier and to their wagons to chase those men-at-arms inside the gate, and the French sallied out in an ambush from the ditches against the English, who were 400 men-at-arms and a hundred arbalesters, who they drove back outside of their barrier and well ahead in the road, where six bannerets of the English were killed and many others; and the English bannerets were Sir Hue Suverin, Sir Guillaume Clinton, Sir John Burley, Sir Fitz Watier, Sir Jehan Franc, and Sir Thomas Trivet. And there were many well wounded among the garrison, but none of them died and none but Robert Gui de Riom was taken; and when he had been disarmed the English who were unhappy about their loss did not take it upon themselves to guard him; so Robert Gui left them and took himself to the ditches and went in there with his companions, who began to laugh. And then the English were much discomfited by the deaths of their barons and their people who they had lost in the skirmishes, and they did not know what to do about it. And a malady of the flux went from bad to worse in their army, which much disemboweled them: for great numbers of their people died of this disease; and they had held the siege before Nantes from vintage up until Christmas, a total of three months and twenty days.

The Deeds of Arms at Vannes (Froissart)

CHAPTER LXIII.—Deeds of arms are performed before the earl of Buckingham between certain French and English knights.

Johnes 1: 631-3; KL 9: 323

At the time when Gauvain Micaille and Joachim Cator performed their combat before the earl of Buckingham and the English lords, certain knights and squires from France had come as spectators to Marchenoir near Blois. At that time Sir Reginald de Touars, lord de Pousanges, a baron of Poitou, had some words with the lord de Vertain, and said he would like to joust with him three courses with the lance and three strokes with the battle-axe. The lord de Vertain, wishing not to refuse, was eager to accommodate him immediately, whatever might be the event: but the earl of Buckingham would not consent, and forbade the knight to think of it at that time.

What had been said relative to this deed of arms was not forgotten by the two knights. Similar words had passed that same day between a squire from Savoy, called the bastard Clarins, and Edward Beauchamp, son of Sir Robert Beauchamp; and also between Sir Tristan de la Jaille and Sir Jean d'Ambreticourt; Sir Jean de Châteaumorand, and Jannequin Clinton; and le Gallois d'Aunay and

Sir William Clinton; between Sir Hoyau d' Araines and Sir William France: but these were all set aside like the first.

During the time the English were quartered in the suburbs of Nantes, these French knights and squires were in the town. The lord de Vertain and the others were requested by the French knights to help them fulfill their engagements while they were before Nantes; but the governors in Nantes would not consent, and excused their friends by saying they were in Nantes as soldiers, entrusted with the guard and defense of the town. Nothing more passed until the earl of Buckingham's army was established in quarters at Vannes, Hennebon, Quimperlé, and Quimpercorentin, when Sir Barrois des Barres, Sir Hoyau d'Araines, and many other knights and squires, came to Chateau Josselin, seven leagues from Vannes, where the constable of France resided. The count de la Marche, with several knights, were also there, who were very glad to see them, and received them handsomely. They informed the constable of all that had passed, and that such and such persons had undertaken deeds of prowess against others of the English. The constable heard this with pleasure, and said, "Send a message to them: we will grant them passports to perform these deeds of arms, if they are willing to come."

Le Gallois d'Aunay and Sir Hoyau d' Araines were the first to say they were ready to perform their engagement of three courses with the spear, on horseback. When Sir William Clinton and Sir William France heard they were called upon by the French to perform their challenges, they rejoiced, and took leave of the earl and barons of England to go thither. They were accompanied by many knights and squires. The English and French jousted very handsomely, and performed their deeds of arms as the rules required. Then Sir Reginald de Touars, Sir Tristan de la Jaille, Sir Jean de Châteaumorand, and the bastard Clarins summoned each of them his knight or squire; that is to say the lord de Vertain, Sir John d'Ambreticourt, Edward Beauchamp, and Jannequin Clinton. These four were so eager for the combat that they wished to go to Château Josselin on the passports of the constable; but the earl of Buckingham, hearing at Vannes the summons from the French, said aloud to the heralds, "You will tell the constable, from the earl of Buckingham, that he [Buckingham] is equally powerful to grant passports to the French as he [the constable] may be to grant them to the English; and to all those who may wish to perform any deeds of arms with his knights, on their arrival at Vannes, he [Buckingham] will, out of his affection to them, give passports, and to all who may choose to accompany them, both for their stay and for their return."

When the constable heard this, he instantly perceived the earl was in the right, and that he wanted to see those deeds of arms: it was but reasonable there should be as many performed at Vannes as had been before him at Château Josselin. The constable therefore said, "the earl of Buckingham speaks like a valiant man and a king's son, and I want that what he says shall be believed: let me know those who may be desirous of accompanying the challengers and we will send for a proper passport." Thirty knights and squires immediately stepped forth: a herald came to Vannes for the passport, which was given to him, sealed by the earl of Buckingham. The three knights who were to perform their deeds of arms set out from Château Josselin, attended by the others, and came to Vannes, where they were lodged in the suburbs, and the English entertained them well. On the morrow, they made preparations for the combat, as it behooved them to do, and advanced to a handsome space, which was large and even, on the outside of the town. Afterwards the earl of Buckingham, the earl of Stafford, the earl of Devonshire, and other barons came, with those who were to engage in this deed of arms: the lord de Vertain against Sir Reginald de Touars, lord de Pousanges; Sir John d'Ambreticourt against Tristan de la Jaille; Edward Beauchamp against the bastard Clarins de Savoy.

The French took their places at one end of the lists, and the English at the other. Those who were to joust were on foot completely armed, with helmets, visors, and provided with lances of good steel from Bordeaux, with which they performed as follows:

First, the lord de Pousanges and the lord de Vertain, two barons of high renown and great courage, advanced towards each other on foot, holding their sharp spears in their hands, with a good pace: they did not spare themselves, but struck their lances lustily against each other while thrusting. The lord de Vertain was hit, without being wounded; but the lord de Pousanges received such a stroke that it pierced through the mail and steel breastplate, and everything underneath, so that the blood gushed out, and it was a great wonder he was not more seriously wounded. They finished their three courses and the other deeds of arms without further mischief, when they retired to rest, and to be spectators of the actions of the others. Sir Jean d'Ambreticourt, who was from Hainault, and Sir Tristan de la Jaille, from Poitou, next advanced, and performed their courses very valiantly, without hurt to either, when they also retired.

Then came the last, Edward Beauchamp and Clarins de Savoy. This bastard was a hardy and strong squire, and much better formed in all his limbs than the Englishman. They ran at each other with a hearty good will: both struck their spears on their adversary's breast; but Edward was knocked down on the ground, which much vexed his countrymen. When he was raised up, he took his spear, and they advanced again to the attack; but the Savoyard drove him backward to the earth, which more enraged the English: they said, Edward's strength was not a match for this Savoyard, and the devil was in him to make him think of jousting against one of such superior force. He was carried off among them, and declared he would not engage further. When Clarins saw this, wishing to finish his course of arms, he said, "Gentlemen, you do not use me well: since Edward wishes not to go on, send me someone with whom I may complete my courses."

The earl of Buckingham wanted to know what Clarins had said, and, when it was reported to him, replied, that the Frenchman had spoken well and valiantly. An English squire then stepped forth, who was since knighted, called Jannequin Finchley, who coming before the earl, kneeled down and entreated his permission to joust with Clarins, to which the earl assented. Jannequin very completely armed himself on the spot: then each of them seized his spear, and thrust at the other, and with such violence that their spears were broken, and the stumps flew over their heads. They began their second attack, and their lances were again broken: so were they in the third. All their lances were broken, which was considered by the lords and spectators as a decisive proof of their gallantry. They then drew their swords, which were strong; and, in six strokes, four of them were broken. They were desirous of fighting with battle-axes, but the earl would not consent to more being done, saying they had sufficiently shown their courage and abilities. Upon this, they both retired; when Sir Jean de Châteaumorand and Jannequin Clinton advanced. This Jannequin was squire of honor to the earl of Buckingham, and the nearest about his person; but he was lightly made and delicate in his form. The earl was uneasy that he should have been matched with one so stout and renowned in arms as Jean de Châteaumorand: notwithstanding, they were put to the trial, and attacked each other most vigorously; but the Englishman could not withstand his opponent, for, in the thrusting, he was very roughly struck to the ground: the earl then said that they were not fairly matched. Some of the earl's people came to Jannequin, and said, "Jannequin, you are not sufficiently strong to continue this combat: and my lord of Buckingham is angry with you for having undertaken it: retire and rest." The Englishman having retired, Jean de Châteaumorand said, "Gentlemen, it seems your squire is too weak: choose another, I beg of you, more to your liking, that I may accomplish the deeds of arms I have engaged to perform; for I shall be very disgracefully treated if I depart hence without having completed them."

The constable and marshal of the army replied, "You speak well, and you shall be gratified." Then the surrounding knights and squires were told that one of them must deliver the lord de Châteaumorand. On these words, Sir William Farrington immediately replied, "Tell him, he shall not depart without fighting: let him go and rest a little in his chair, and he shall soon be delivered; for I will arm myself against him." This answer was very pleasing to Jean de Châteaumorand, who went to his seat to rest. The English knight was soon ready and on the field. They placed themselves opposite each other, and taking their lances, they began a course of jousting on foot with their spears within the four members; for it was esteemed disgraceful to hit any part but the body.

They advanced to each other with great courage, completely armed, the visor down and helmet tightly fixed on. Jean de Châteaumorand gave the knight such a blow on the helmet that Sir William Farrington staggered a little, because his foot slipped: he kept his spear stiffly with both hands, and, lowering it by the stumble he made, struck Jean de Châteaumorand on the thighs; he could not avoid it; and the spearhead passed through, and came out the length of one's hand on the other side. Jean de Châteaumorand reeled with the blow, but did not fall.

The English knights were much enraged at this, and said, it was infamously done. The Englishman excused himself by saying, he was extremely sorry for it; and if he had thought it would have so happened at the commencement of the combat, he would never have undertaken it: but that he could not help it, for his foot slipped from the violence of the blow he had received. Thus the matter was passed over. The French, after taking leave of the earl and other lords, departed, carrying with them Jean de Châteaumorand in a litter, to Château

Josselin, whence they had come, and where he was in great danger of his life from the effects of this wound.

These deeds of arms being finished, each retired to his home; the English to Vannes, the French to Château Josselin.

Deeds of Arms at Vannes (Cabaret)

XLIII. How the earl of Buckingham removed himself from Nantes, and how the fifteen English did not perform their arms with fifteen French.

CBD 127-9

Charles, King of France, in honor of his coronation, made many knights, of whom many he had in Nantes, who with their companions strongly held it against the English. The earl of Buckingham who saw the infirmity of his people and that he had no profit from holding his siege anymore before Nantes, had planned to leave for this reason; but he delayed some, because fifteen men-at-arms of the house of the duke of Bourbon had proposed a battle on an island near Nantes against fifteen other men-at-arms English, from the house of the earl of Buckingham, to fight to the end, and that there should be no judges but only two heralds, one from France and one from England. This thing was promised and sworn that the English defaulted as you will hear. And this enterprise cost the duke of Bourbon 3000 francs in harness and equipment which he ordered for his people, every day, for the space of three weeks; and the fifteen who were of the house of the duke of Bourbon did not fail to demand that the English hold this battle, but the English sent them messages and said: "Wait, wait, we will tell you in good time." The earl of Buckingham, seeing that he was losing many of his Englishman to the stomach flux, broke camp one evening with all of his people, and on the next day in the evening the fifteen Englishmen sent by a herald to the fifteen French of the house of the duke of Bourbon that they were not at all able to hold that battle then, but they wished to go to Vannes, where their master the earl had gone and accomplish their arms then. The fifteen of the duke of Bourbon gave no other response but to say to the herald that if the duke of Brittany wished to give them good security that they should do and accomplish them there. They left the siege of Nantes without gaining any profit, and the earl of Buckingham and his Englishman rode to Vannes. And after them the French captains sallied forth: Sir Jehan de Châteaumorand, Sir Le Barrois, Sir Pierre de Bueil, and the Marshal of Savoy, who well had 800 men-at-arms who skirmished and kept close to the English, and gained much from their carriage before they got to Vannes. And the French withdrew to Château Josselin, where the lord of Clisson, the new constable of France, had come, and those of the garrison of Nantes demanded leave to go so they could return to their masters. The constable refused, and asked them to wait for the English to disembark. At that time the fifteen of the house the duke of Bourbon, who were returned to Nantes in their station with the others, sent to the fifteen English that they were prepared to accomplish their promise and that they should send to them good assurance from the earl of Buckingham their master and from the duke of Brittany and then they would come willingly. So a herald carried the safe conducts to Sir Jean de Châteaumorand, to Sir Le Barrois, and to their companions, and that with them they were able to have forty gentlemen to accompany them, and they willingly received the safe conducts believing that the fifteen Frenchmen would certainly not come; but notwithstanding the safe conducts the fifteen sent Cordellier de Gironne, a squire of the squires of the King of France, for the assurance of the earl of Buckingham and the duke of Brittany who brought it, and the fifteen companions went with Cordellier to Vannes to the duke of Brittany and to the earl of Buckingham who were there present, and notified them that those who had made a promise had come all ready to accomplish it the next day after mass.

XLIV. How five noble Frenchmen performed arms at Vannes, against five noble Englishmen and what happened.

CBD 130-2

The earl of Buckingham, seeing that this was in earnest undertook serious consultation with the duke of Brittany about what should be done. And the response which the earl of Buckingham made was that his people were not up to the mark, and it had been a year since he left England and also that he and his people had been at siege before Nantes for three months, for which reason their harness was very deteriorated. For this reason he was not in favor of performing arms especially to extremities but he had thought to give his advice to some of his servants that if there were any from the household of the duke of Bourbon who wished to perform specified arms, to this he agreed willingly. So the companions of the agreement were much amazed and infuriated thinking that they would not fight at all. So they decided that they should not hold to them but it would be good to do something of the sort for which they had come there and so they should take what the English were offering. The arms which the English wished to perform were five blows of the lance, five of the sword, five of the axe, five of the dagger, all on foot; and it was granted to them. And the next day early in the morning there were but five Englishmen who wished to perform arms and from the people of the duke of Bourbon another five: namely Jean de Châteaumorand, Sir Le Barrois, the bastard of Clarins, the viscount of Aunay, Sir Tristan de la Jaille; and the five English were Sir Walter Cloppeton, Edward de Beauchamp, Sir Thomas de Hennefort, Brisselai, and Sir Jehan de Traro. All the companions present on the field where the duke of Brittany and the earl of Buckingham were accompanied by their people. The first of the French to perform arms was Jean de Châteaumorand against Walter Cloppeton, an Englishman, of which they were not able to do more than three blows of the lance on foot, for Sir Walter Cloppeton was wounded by the lance right through, between the lames and the piece, and it passed through as he fell to the earth and for those two there were only these three blows, for Cloppeton was carried off. Sir Le Barrois, who was armed, entered the field to perform arms against his companion, Thomas de Hennefort, who entered the field likewise and they did their five blows with the lance very chivalrously; and when it came to swords and they attacked, at the first blow of the sword Barrois wounded the Englishman between the piece and the gardebras and damaged the mail and pierced the shoulder completely so that it was necessary to lead off the Englishman without performing more arms. Then came the bastard of Clarins and Edward Beauchamp and when it came to combat with lances Edward Beauchamp turned his shoulder a little, so much so that the bastard of Clarins twice knocked him to the ground with two blows of the lance, notwithstanding that he was large of body and a good gentleman. And then the Englishmen said that Beauchamp was ***dronch,*** that is to say, drunk. They picked him up and led him away. Then Sir Tristan de la Jaille came to his English companion and they accomplished all of their arms up to the axes; and when they came to strike Sir Tristan knocked down his Englishman with the second axe blow, and badly wounded him and that was that. The Viscount d'Aunay came into the field to fight his companion, who performed his arms beautifully, but the Viscount wounded the Englishmen with last blow of the lance, between the avant-bras and the garde-bras, and pierced the arm right through, so that he did no more. And so were the arms accomplished that day in which the five noble men, the French companions, had the better of it, and the five noble Englishmen the worse as you have seen above.[2]

XLV How after the arms were accomplished Sir Guillaume Farintonne, an Englishman and Jean de Châteaumorand fought and what happened; and how the knight was put in prison and how Châteaumorand said some fine words.

CBD 132-5

2 Items of armor mentioned:
avant-bras = covering the lower arm
gardebras = covering the upper arm
lames = bands of steel
pièce = breastplate?

The duke of Brittany and the earl of Buckingham, who had seen these arms, retired to their houses, and the French disarmed themselves; and because it was almost night the duke of Brittany sent one of his knights, the maître d' hôtel, to summon them to supper with him. They conceded it to him as they had been in his city and all those who had performed arms came to supper and the duke of Brittany highly honored them, making them all sit at his table and serving them very grandly. And after the removal of the table there came a knight, fair and grand, named Guillaume Farrington, who urged Châteaumorand to perform arms that Sir Walter Cloppeton, his cousin german, had hardly been able to accomplish. So Châteaumorand agreed with him that if it pleased the duke of Brittany, but he did not wish to allow it and it infuriated him most feloniously against his English knight, who had come to make demands at his table. But Châteaumorand begged so much to the duke of Brittany that the next day at sunrise he was armed in the field against the one who had demanded it, to accomplish this, and more which he had not demanded, because it was necessary for his companions to mount up the next day. And when they were together in the field the English knight had no armor at all on his legs for he had a disease in one knee, on account of which he was not able to arm himself there, and they sent via Cordellier de Gironne to urge Châteaumorand that they should not have more armor on the legs and they should guarantee not to strike at uncovered areas. This having been done the two knights in the field struck lances and with that stroke did their duty well; at the second blow they came strongly together, and the Englishmen, Sir Guillaume, struck Sir Jean de Châteaumorand on the arms and Châteaumorand struck the Englishmen under the cincture, so much so that Sir Guillaume Farrington fell to one knee, and put a hand to the ground; and at the third blow of the lances they came in contact strongly against each other but when it came to the clash Sir Guillaume lowered his lance and crouched a little with the result that he pierced Sir Jean de Châteaumorand right through the thigh, and it was advisable to carry him to his hôtel; on account of this blow there was a great cry from the company present seeing that the English knight had promised not to make an attempt by arms on uncovered areas, especially on the legs. And then the duke of Brittany and the earl of Buckingham who had seen this impropriety had the Englishman Sir Guillaume taken, and disarmed to his little pourpoint and went to have him hurled in prison and they said to Barrois, cousin German of Châteaumorand:

"Go to Châteaumorand and tell him that we are very unhappy and indeed infuriated that this knight has failed to do what he had promised and we are delivering him to Châteaumorand to be his prisoner, to put him to such ransom as pleases him and, between you his friends, if Châteaumorand dies you can do what you like to that knight." This was considered very just on the part of the lords to maintain their sureties and safe conducts. So Châteaumorand heard the response from Barrois and Cordellier de Gironne, to which Châteaumorand answered that he thanked heartily the earl of Buckingham and the duke of Brittany for the good reason and justice which he found in their lordships and that he would prefer that Farrington had damaged his honor over him than that he, Châteaumorand, should have damaged his over him. "And when you inform me that he ought to be my prisoner I thank you humbly and please you to know that when we came from our side before you to perform arms with your surety and safe conduct neither my companions nor I came motivated by avarice nor covetousness and it would turn to my dishonor to wish take ransom from your knight for which I beg you to let him out from prison and do what you please, for the deed of arms involves risk. And you well know that the duke of Bourbon to whom we belong gives us what we need and he, who sends us out in the world to acquire honor, would be discontented with this covetousness." And the Englishmen and the Bretons found these words to be very honorable and the earl of Buckingham sent to Châteaumorand a goblet of gold and 150 nobles [a gold coin]; but Châteaumorand returned the gold coins to him, letting him know that he had enough money for his affairs. So he kept the goblet to drink from for the sake of his honor. At that time Châteaumorand told his companions that they should not delay riding back for him. For he did not think himself in such bad shape that he could not follow their trot.

Nicholas Clifford and Jean Boucinel (Froissart)

CHAPTER LXIV.—The duke of Brittany makes his peace with the king of France.— The English return home.—A combat between an English and a French squire.

Johnes 1: 633-6 ; KL 9: 330

After these deeds of arms were performed, during the residence of the earl of Buckingham at Vannes, nothing happened worth mentioning. The English, as I have before said, were quartered at Vannes, Hennebon, Quimperlé and Quimpercorentin: they passed the whole winter in Brittany as well as they could. Very many of them were ill, and suffered much from the badness and scarcity of provision; as did also their horses, for their foragers could not find anything in the open country, which at that season is always bare. The French had taken every precaution that the enemy should not be very comfortable. The English were in this perilous state for some time; for the French were so strong in the surrounding garrisons, they dared not make any excursions. Some provisions came to them by sea from Cornwall, Guernsey and the Isle of Wight, which were a great relief to them; otherwise they and their cavalry would have perished through famine.

During this time, the four Breton barons remained at Paris on behalf of the duke, negotiating a peace between him and the king. He did not oppose it; for he saw clearly that he could not keep the promises he had made the English, unless he would lose his dukedom. It was the intention of the earl of Buckingham and his barons to pass the winter in the town of Vannes as well as they could, and in the summer to return to France to continue the war: he had written a full account of his situation and intentions to the king of England and to the duke of Lancaster. The king and his council, having approved of this plan, ordered him to carry it into execution, adding, that at the proper season, English reinforcements should be sent to Normandy and land at Cherbourg; and those two armies, being united in Normandy, might be able to perform some decisive actions in France.

The king of France, his uncles and council, foresaw all that might happen, having been duly informed of the intended plans: they said, in their secret councils, that if the duke of Brittany, or any of his principal towns, were at enmity with the realm, and united with the English force, France would have, for a time, too heavy a burden to bear. For this reason, the four barons from Brittany, who represented the duke and managed his affairs very well, had thrown out these doubts: in particular, they had confided to the duke of Anjou, at that time regent of France, who having a grand expedition in his head, and intending within two years at the farthest to march to Apulia and Calabria, would not have chosen that the kingdom of France should be disturbed, nor his expedition put off. He was therefore strongly inclined to make peace with the duke of Brittany, that he might become a good Frenchman, loyal in faith and homage to the king of France. The articles of peace were now discussed by the four barons: it was settled that the duke might, without blame, assist the English with vessels to return to their own country. The duke was permitted to add to his ordinances; that if those who had come from the garrison of Cherbourg to serve under the earl of Buckingham wished to return thither by land, they should have passports from the king and constable to march through France, but unarmed, and any knights or squires from England who might be desirous of accompanying them: and that, when the English had left Brittany, the duke was to come to the king and his uncles at Paris, and acknowledge himself vassal by faith and homage to the king, in such way as a duke of Brittany owes to his lord, the king of France. All these articles were properly drawn out and sealed, and carried to the duke of Brittany, who at that time was resident at Sucinio, near to Vannes. He agreed to what his ambassadors had done, but much against his inclination: for he knew he could not do it, without incurring the greatest ill-will from the English.

When the earl of Buckingham and his knights heard that the duke of Brittany had made peace with France, they were greatly enraged and very indignant, saying, he had sent for them and made them come to Brittany, where he had never performed any one of the promises he had sworn to; for which reason they pronounced him void of loyalty. Shortly after, the duke visited the earl of Buckingham and his barons at Vannes, when he openly explained to them the treaty his people had made for him, and which it behooved him to agree to, for otherwise he should lose his whole duchy. Upon this, high words passed between the earl and his barons with the duke; but the duke humbled and excused himself as much as possible, for he was conscious that he had been in some sort to blame. It was, however, necessary to come to terms, in order that the English might leave Brittany. The earl then gave notice to the city of Vannes, that if any of his men were indebted to the inhabitants, they should come forward, when they would be paid. He gave back to the magistrates the keys of the town, and thanked them for their attentions to him.

The earl was supplied with vessels at Vannes, Hennebon and Quimperlé, and wherever else they had been quartered, on paying for them: he left Vannes the eleventh day of April, in battle-array, with banners displayed, and thus marched to the haven. The duke of Brittany, Sir Alain de la Houssaye, the lord de Montboursier, Sir Stephen Guyon, Sir William de Tresiquidi, Sir Geoffry de Kerimel and others of his council, came thither: they sent to inform the earl, who was in his vessel, that the duke wanted to speak with him; but the earl refused to come, and sent the lord Latimer and lord Thomas Percy. These two had a conference with the duke for three hours, and, after long debates, consented to request the earl, that before he set sail, he would on another day have a conversation with the duke: they then went to his ship, and related to the earl all that had passed.

About midnight, on the return of the tide, the wind became favorable; and the mariners asked the earl what were his intentions. The earl, who wished not for any further conferences, said, "Weigh your anchor and set your sails, and let us be gone." This was soon done; and thus did the English sail from the harbor of Vannes for England. All the others did the same in their different ports, and collected together at sea.

We will now speak of certain knights and squires who returned to Cherbourg by land, and relate what befell them on their road. The constable of France, who at that time resided at Château Josselin, seven leagues from Vannes, had granted passports to some English and Navarrese knights of the garrison of Cherbourg, who had served under the earl of Buckingham. Among others were Sir John Harlestone, governor of Cherbourg, Sir Evan Fitzwarren, Sir William Clinton and Sir John Burley. They set out from Vannes, following the road to Château Josselin, for it was in their route. On their arrival, they took up their quarters in the town below the castle, not intending more than to dine and continue their journey. When they had dismounted at the inn, like travelers who wished to take a break, the knights and squires of the castle came to visit them as brother-soldiers, who always see each other with pleasure, particularly the French and English. Among the French, there was a squire of great renown in arms, who belonged to Jean de Bourbon, count de la Marche, the nearest to his person of all his squires, and whom he loved the most: his name was Jean Boucinel. He had formerly been in garrison in Valogne with Sir William des Bordes, and in his expedition against Cherbourg. During that time, he had often had words with an English squire, called Nicholas Clifford, who was then present, respecting a deed of arms. In the course of the conversation which these French knights and squires held at the inn with the English, Jean Boucinel, recollecting Clifford, cried out, "Nicholas Clifford! Ah! Nicholas, Nicholas, we have often wished and sought to perform a deed of arms; but we never could find fit opportunity or place for it. Now, as we are here before my lord constable and those gentlemen, let us perform it: I therefore demand from you three courses with a lance."

"Jean," replied Nicholas, "you know that we are here but as travelers on our road, under the passport of my lord constable: what you ask from me cannot be done now, for I am not the principal in the passport, but under the command of these knights whom you see: if I were to stay behind, they would set out without me."

"Ha, Nicholas, do not make such excuses as these: let your friends depart, if they please, for I give you my promise, that as soon as our arms have been accomplished, I will conduct you myself within the gates of Cherbourg without loss or peril, as I can depend on my lord constable's good will."

Nicholas said, " Now suppose it to be as you say, and that I place my confidence in being safely conducted by you; yet you see we are travelling through the country without arms of any sort: therefore, if I were willing to arm myself, I have not wherewithal to do so."

Jean replied, "You shall not excuse yourself that way, for I will tell you what I will do: I have plenty of arms at my command, and will order different sorts to be brought to the place where we shall perform our arms; and, when all are laid out, you shall examine them, and consider which will suit you best: for I will leave the choice to you, and, when you shall have chosen, I will then arm myself."

When Nicholas saw himself so earnestly pressed, he was ashamed that those present should have heard it, and thought, that since Jean made such handsome offers, he could not in honor refuse them; for Jean still added, "Make whatever arrangements you please, I will agree to them sooner than we should not have a deed of arms."

Nicholas then said, he would consider it; and, before his departure he would let him know what he had decided; adding, "if it will not be possible for me to comply with your request here, and if my lords, under whom I am, are unwilling to assent to it, on my return to Cherbourg, if you will come to Valogne, and inform me of your arrival, I will immediately hurry over and deliver you from your engagement."

"No, no," said Jean, "no excuses: I have offered you such handsome proposals, that you cannot in honor depart without doing this deed of arms which I demand of you." Nicholas was more enraged than before; for he thought, and true it was, that he, by such a speech, greatly outraged his honor. Upon this, the French returned to the castle, and the English to their inn, where they dined.

When these knights had got to the castle, you may suppose they were not silent about the words which had passed between Jean Boucinel and Nicholas Clifford, with the result that the constable heard about it. He considered a short time; and, when the knights and squires of the country who were with him begged him to use his influence to make sure that this combat was fought, he willingly promised it. The English knights and squires, wishing to pursue their journey after dinner, went to the castle to wait on the constable; for he was to give them seven knights to escort them the whole road, through Brittany and Normandy, as far as Cherbourg.

When they were arrived at the castle, the constable received them very amicably, and then said, "I put you all under arrest, and forbid you to depart hence today: tomorrow morning, after mass, you shall witness the combat between your squire and ours, and then you shall dine with me. After dinner you shall set out, and I will give you good guides to conduct you to Cherbourg." They complied with his requests, and, having drunk his wine, returned to their inn. Now the two squires consulted together, for it was settled they should in the morning engage without fail.

When morning came, they both heard mass, confessed themselves, and mounted their horses; the French being on one side, and the English on the other. They rode together to a smooth plain on the outside of the castle, where they dismounted. Jean Boucinel had provided there two suits of armor, according to his promise, which were good and strong, as the occasion demanded: having displayed them, he told the English squire to make the first choice. "No," said the Englishman, "I will not choose: you shall have the choice." Jean was therefore forced to choose first, which he did, and armed himself completely (in doing which he was assisted), as a good man-at-arms should be. Nicholas did the same.

When they were both armed, they grasped their spears, well made with Bordeaux steel and of the same length; and each took the position proper for him to run his course, with their helmets and visors closed. They then advanced, and, when they approached pretty near, they lowered their spears, aiming them to hit each other. At the first onset, Nicholas Clifford struck Jean Boucinel with his spear on the upper part of his breast; but the point slipped off the steel breastplate, and pierced the hood, which was of good mail, and, entering his neck, cut the jugular vein, and passed quite through, breaking off at the shaft with the head; so that the truncheon remained in the neck of the squire, who was killed, as you may suppose. The English squire passed on to his chair, where he seated himself. The French lords, who had seen the stroke and the broken spear in Boucinel's neck, hastened to him: they immediately took off his helmet, and drew out the spear. On its being extracted, he turned himself about without uttering a word, and fell down dead. The English squire hurried to his relief, crying out to have the blood staunched, but could not arrive before he expired. Nicholas Clifford was then exceedingly vexed, for having by ill fortune slain a valiant and good man-at-arms. All who at that time could have seen the despair of the count de la Marche, who had such an affection for his deceased squire, would surely have much pitied him; he was in the greatest distress, for he esteemed him above all others.

The constable was present, and endeavored to comfort him, saying that such things were to be expected in similar combats. "It has turned out unfortunate for our squire, but the Englishman could not help it." He then addressed himself to the English, "Come, come to dinner, for it is ready." The constable led them, as I may say, against their will to the castle to dinner, for they wished not to go there on account of the death of the Frenchman.

The count de la Marche most tenderly bewailed his squire as he viewed his corpse. Nicholas Clifford directly retired to his lodgings, and would not by any means dine at the castle, because of the great vexation he was in for this death and also on account of his relations and friends: but the constable had him sought out, and he had to comply. On his arrival, the constable said, "In truth, Nicholas, I can very well believe, and I see by your looks, that you are very upset at the death of Jean Boucinel; but I acquit you of it, for it was no fault of yours, and, as God is my judge, if I had been in the situation you were in, you have done nothing more than I would have done, as it is better to hurt one's enemy than to be hurt by him. Such are the vicissitudes of arms."

They then seated themselves at table, and these lords dined at their ease. After they had finished their repast, and drank their wine, the constable called the lord le Barrois des Barres, and said to him, "Barrois, prepare yourself: I want you to conduct these Englishmen as far as Cherbourg, and that you have opened to them every town and castle, so that they are given whatever they shall be in need of."

Barrois replied, "My lord, I shall cheerfully obey your orders."

The English, then, taking leave of the constable and the knights with him, came to their lodgings, where everything was packed up and ready. They mounted their horses, departed from Château Josselin, and rode straight to Pontorson and Mont St. Michel. They were under the escort of that gallant knight Barrois des Barres, who never left them in Brittany or Normandy, until they had arrived in Cherbourg. In this manner did the army of the earl of Buckingham left France by sea and by land.

Bibliography

Texts and Translations

Froissart, Jean. *Chronicles,* trans. Thomas Johnes. 2 vols. London, 1862.

Abbreviated "Johnes."

———. *Œuvres,* ed. Kervyn de Lettenhove. 25 vols. Brussels, 1867–77.

Abbreviated "KL."

La Chronique du bon duc Loys de Bourbon, ed. A. M. Chazaud. Paris, 1876.

Abbreviated "CBD."

Translations are mine except where noted. In the case of Froissart's *Chronicles,* however, I have very closely followed Thomas Johnes' translation; most of the changes I have made are modernizations of syntax and vocabulary. I, of course, am alone responsible for the accuracy of the translations and broader interpretations offered here.

Secondary Works

Barber, Richard and Juliet Barker. *Tournaments: Jousts, chivalry and pageants in the Middle Ages.* Woodbridge: Boydell Press, 1989.

Crouch, David. *The Birth of Nobility: Constructing aristocracy in England and France, 950-1300.* London: Longman, 2005.

Kaeuper, Richard W. *Chivalry and Violence in Medieval Europe.* Oxford: Oxford University Press, 1999.

Keen, Maurice. *Chivalry.* New Haven: Yale University Press, 1984.

Muhlberger, Steven. *Charny's Men-at-Arms: Questions concerning the joust, tournaments and war.* Wheaton, IL: Freelance Academy Press, 2014.

———. *Deeds of Arms: Formal combats in the late fourteenth century.* Highland Village, TX: Chivalry Bookshelf, 2005.

———. *Jousts and Tournaments: Charny and chivalric sport in fourteenth-century France.* Union City: Chivalry Bookshelf, 2003.

Palmer, J. J. N. *England, France and Christendom 1377-99.* London: Routledge and Kegan Paul, 1972.

Sumption, Jonathan. *The Hundred Years War III: Divided houses.* Philadelphia: University of Pennsylvania Press, 2009.

Taylor, Craig. *Chivalry and the Ideals of Knighthood in France during the Hundred Years War.* Cambridge: Cambridge University Press, 2013.